Published by the Royal Society for the Protection of Birds
The Lodge, Sandy, Bedfordshire SG19 2DL

Typesetting: Bedford Typesetters Ltd.
Origination: Saxon Photolitho Ltd.
Printer: GCW Colourprint
Compiled by Rob Hume
Designed by Philip Cottier

ISBN no: 0/903138/19/0

A YEAR OF BIRD LIFE

CONTENTS

❝ One of the best things about birdwatching is that you can do it at any time of the year, wherever you happen to be. At first you will probably want to find out what species they are, but soon you will try to understand their behaviour, to know how they work, what they feed on and how they fit into the natural world.

Bird Life, the bi-monthly magazine of the Young Ornithologists' Club (YOC), helps you to do this. Each issue has many colourful articles, written and illustrated by experts, to tell you about birds and other animals and plants. This is a selection of some of our popular features over the past few years.

There is a chapter for each month, spotlighting a common bird and with a nature notebook of a typical day's birdwatching. The 'Focus on' series examines one particular subject a little more closely.

If you are already a YOC member, this book will be a bonus. If you do not belong to the YOC, I hope very much that this will tempt you to join. (Details are on page 128 and you can send for a free copy of *Bird Life*.) The YOC is a very special club. Its members can take part in all sorts of activities — local group meetings and outings, holidays, competitions, projects and fun days. YOC members want to do more than just look at birds; they want to study them and help with their conservation. That is what ornithology is all about. **,,**

Peter Holden
YOC National Organiser

JANUARY

January is the coldest month of the year, but don't let that put you off birdwatching. A winter walk can bring some exciting surprises. Sudden changes in the weather mean that large numbers of birds have to roam around the country in search of food. Fresh snow will give you a marvellous chance to look at the tracks and signs left by birds and mammals.

LOOK AT Blackbirds

Everyone knows the blackbird — a garden bird, present all year over the whole of the British Isles. But if more than usual are visiting your garden this winter, then it is likely that many of them are continental visitors avoiding bad conditions further north or east.

Roger Wilmshurst (Bruce Coleman)

Key facts

Scientific name: *Turdus merula*
Key features: male all black, orange-yellow bill. Female dark brown with paler throat.
Where seen: gardens, woodlands, hillsides, commons.
Nests: in hedges, bushes, in sheds.
Food: fruit, berries, seeds, worms, insects.
Voice: fluty song. Call note "tchook, tchook, tchook".

Although one of our commonest birds, with over ten million pairs breeding, blackbirds are surprisingly often misidentified. The glossy black male with its orange-yellow bill is easy to recognise — but the brown female, which often has a speckled breast, can be mistaken for a dark song thrush. Immature blackbirds are particularly confusing in late summer when they gradually moult into adult plumage and, for a time, are dark brown with a ginger-brown head. Confusion can also arise over partial albino birds with white feathers on the head, neck, wings or tail. Some blackbirds may have a white patch on the breast which makes them look similar to ring ouzels.

Male blackbirds are very territorial and announce their territories by singing from high, conspicuous song posts. The loud, clear song begins in February and continues until July when it stops completely — apart from young males occasionally singing in autumn. Any intruder in a territory is quickly seen off, and a bird will often attack its own reflection in windows, car hub caps and mirrors, thinking it to be an intruder.

A large part of a bird's life is spent searching for food and blackbirds are often seen standing still, with their head on one side, watching and listening for worms. On a hot summer's day, they often 'sun' themselves on the ground with their wings outstretched, feathers fluffed out and their beaks wide open. During the autumn and early winter fruit and berries become their main food, but during severe winter weather many would not survive if it were not for extra food put out by humans.

nature notebook

by Audrey Lincoln

Reservoirs, gravel pits and other inland lakes are good places to see lots of birds in winter. Large numbers of mallard, pochard, shoveler, teal and tufted duck are often present, with smaller numbers of pintail, goldeneye and goosander. You may also see large numbers of coot and great crested grebes. Always scan open water carefully because hiding among the flocks of birds there may be a smew, a scaup or one of the three rarer species of grebes (red-necked, Slavonian and black-necked).

You may be surprised to see a grey squirrel searching in the snow for nuts that it stored in autumn. Grey squirrels do not hibernate for the whole winter,

but sleep for several days and then wake to search for food. They will often raid bird tables and even dustbins for food.

Other unusual bird table visitors are often seen in very cold weather. Siskins, for example, usually feed on alder seeds, but will visit bird tables to feed on nuts when natural food is scarce. Many blue tits, great tits, greenfinches and other small birds will visit your garden if you provide food and fresh water every day.

choose tall trees, usually elms, but since the decline of these trees due to Dutch elm disease, they now often nest in other trees including oaks and ash.

On warm sunny days the first brimstone butterflies emerge to fly. The male is bright yellow, and the female is a paler creamy colour. They hibernate among ivy leaves, which protect them from the worst of the cold and wet.

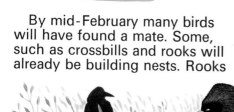

By mid-February many birds will have found a mate. Some, such as crossbills and rooks will already be building nests. Rooks

Michael Hodgson

FOCUS on birds and weather

by Irene Allen

Weather movements

Herons may fly to coasts and estuaries when the weather is bad. Here, it is easier to find food because salty water stays unfrozen when freshwater streams and lakes are iced over. Kingfishers, dippers and great crested grebes may do this too.

As fronts of cold weather move across the country, freezing the ground and making food-finding difficult, flocks of lapwings and skylarks take to the air and fly away to the warmer west and south to find unfrozen feeding grounds.

Miles out!

Migrating birds often have to battle against the weather. Gales can blow them right off course and lead to birds from North America, like this **long-billed dowitcher**, turning up in Britain, or seabirds such as Manx shearwaters or puffins falling exhausted miles inland. Cloud too can be disastrous;

G D Plage (Bruce Coleman Ltd)

J B & S Bottomley

migrating birds rely on landmarks and the stars to find their way and when these are blotted out they can get hopelessly lost.

In bad weather, birds migrating across sea may stop off on oil rigs, boats or lighthouses. Those near to land may stop and rest in large numbers and this is called a 'fall' of birds. The usual species in a fall are warblers, chats and flycatchers. Swifts have been seen hanging from walls in huge clumps, huddled together for warmth.

Changing diets

In bad winter weather **meadow pipits** may turn up in gardens and towns seeking food from man. Skylarks, moorhens and green woodpeckers may also feed in gardens in hard weather. Many birds change their diet when their usual food runs out or is buried in ice or snow. But some do not seem able to change and may starve. Hardest hit are small birds like wrens and goldcrests.

An ill wind

Probably the only birds to benefit from bad winter weather are carrion feeders. **Carrion crows** can feast on all the small birds and animals killed by the bad weather.

Peter Rowarth

G I Bernard (OSF)

Many of our birds have headed south for the winter

The house martins which nested under the eaves in your town or village — perhaps on your own house — and the swallows from the local farm or allotment sheds will probably be flying over the big animals of Africa. The very same swallow which you saw perched beside a house sparrow last summer may, if it survived the dangerous journey south, now be next to a brilliant bird like a lilac-breasted roller or a red-billed hornbill, species never seen in Europe. It could be looking down on a lion or zebra, or flying around a black rhinoceros in search of insects disturbed by the huge animal.

Most swallows winter south of the Equator. Some 220 million leave Europe for Africa, where they act just as they do here, flying low over open ground especially around large animals. They also take advantage of bush fires which force insects into the open, and gather round swarms of termites. Sometimes tens of thousands — even half a million — roost together in huge reedbeds. In South Africa our swallows outnumber the local breeding species of swallows and martins. Most British-bred birds winter in one area of south-east South Africa but in recent years they have spread westwards. Nearly all those from Germany are 1,600 km north of ours in a much warmer area. British ones can be caught out and killed by a sudden cold spell because they are so far south. Yet they always keep separate and stick to their traditional areas.

House martins are a bit of a mystery — it is thought that 20 to 90 million must winter in Africa, yet they are rarely seen. In some areas they have been noted flying at very high levels, above the local wire-tailed swallows, striped swallows and other similar African species.

Most British chiffchaffs winter near the Mediterranean, but the familiar willow warblers from your local park or wood go to central and southern Africa. Except in December and January they frequently sing — perhaps the willow warbler whose song is so much enjoyed in England is now singing in an area of hot thorny bush, with monkeys and mongooses close by.

Robert Gillmor

THEY NOW?

What is life like for them now?

Illustrated by Robert Gillmor

Sedge warblers are common in central and southern Africa in reeds, long grass, sedges or bushes over water. Reed warblers are found further east, in swamps or drier grassland, even in crops and bushes. They may see crowned cranes, huge marabou storks, African fish eagles and jacanas (like huge-footed, brightly coloured moorhens) and hippopotamuses, resting leopards or even crocodiles. Quite a change from their nesting areas amongst the reeds of an English marsh!

Our yellow wagtails will be much further west in Africa, in Sene-Gambia where it is mostly very hot, dusty and dry. They behave much the same as they do here, but, instead of feeding amongst the cattle in watermeadows with starlings and lapwings, they are chasing flies amongst the long-horned African cattle alongside cattle egrets. They will need to keep a wary eye out for red-necked falcons and shikras (like small sparrowhawks) but the huge hooded and white-backed vultures overhead would be harmless despite their appearance.

Turtle doves also winter in Africa — sometimes tens of thousands roost together through the hot nights in acacia thickets alive with the noise of tropical insects. One roost was shared with 50 tawny eagles, 15 fish eagles and hundreds of black kites!

Some birds will really have been on safari by the time they return next spring! But many return to exactly the same garden or wood as before.

Think of the common sandpiper, too, which nested beside a Welsh stream or by the stony shores of a Scottish lake. Last autumn it would have set off south down to the Mediterannean and beyond, leaving behind the sheep, the neighbouring wagtails and dippers and the cool summer evenings.

Now it will be in Africa, where common sandpipers spend the winter on streams, mountain torrents, even on puddles in roads. Our bird, perhaps, is running along a muddy west African creek in the mangrove swamps, amongst fiddler crabs, reef herons and sacred ibises, as well as native fishermen. Or it could be beside a lake in Natal with jacanas, egrets, malachite kingfishers and noisy, spectacular blacksmith plovers!

To most of us, such places are to be read about in books or watched on television; but the birds, which know no boundaries, travel from Africa to Britain and back again every year of their lives.

Robert Gillmor

FEBRUARY

As the hours of daylight begin to lengthen, you can watch for signs of nesting behaviour. You may see large, noisy flocks of magpies chasing each other through the trees. These flocks are sometimes called 'magpie marriages' and allow birds to find a mate. If one bird of a pair dies early in the nesting season, a magpie marriage often forms in the area soon afterwards and the remaining bird finds a new partner.

LOOK AT TUFTED DUCKS

Isn't he neat and tidy! A male (drake) tufted duck is black and white, with a purple gloss on the head and a bill. Notice the droopy tuft on the back of the head, which no other duck has. Compare him with the scaup and goldeneye in your bird books.

The female (duck), like the drake, is round and dumpy with a large, round head, she even has a trace of the tuft. When they fly, both sexes show a long stripe of white along the wing so you should not confuse them with pochards.

Tufted ducks float on the water like corks but easily dive under to feed. They are really quite common in the winter, and are often seen with pochards (which are more sleepy during the day).

Up to 4-5,000 pairs nest in Britain, with almost half as many again in Ireland. Only in north Scotland, Wales and the south-west of England are they rare nesters. They usually lay seven to 12 eggs. They breed later than most ducks and broods of young are not often seen before July. Then you will see lines of very dark ducklings following their mother across the water.

When you watch tufted ducks, see how often they dive and how long they stay under. Do they ever bring food to the surface? Check to see whether there are more males than females — does this change during the winter? You can do this even at the local park lake, as tufted ducks are often quite tame and easy to watch.

Key facts

Scientific name: *Aythya fuligula*
Key features: Male black and white with tuft on back of head. Female brown with trace of tuft. White stripe along wing.
When seen: All year.
Where seen: Ponds, lakes, gravel pits.
Nests: Near water, in long grass.
Voice: Drake has a soft whistle, female a growling call.
Food: Molluscs, crustaceans, insects, small fish.

nature notebook

February fields
by Nicholas Hammond

The place — a common on the edge of a small town. For hundreds of years it has been grazed by cattle, sheep and horses. Along three of the sides are hedges. One of them is the old parish boundary. It is thick and contains several species of trees and shrubs. It gives excellent cover from which to watch the birds on the common.

The time — a Sunday afternoon in early February.

The weather — cold and bright with a moderate breeze.

The birds — 120+ black-headed gulls, already one has the chocolate-coloured head that more usually comes in the spring. They are resting with their heads into the wind. Near them is a flock of 120+ lapwings, their bodies hunched and their crests blown backwards. Smaller than the lapwings are the golden plover, about 50 of them. They are less colourful and only with binoculars can I see the gold on their backs.

At the hedge bottom are clumps of glossy, arrow-shaped leaves belonging to cuckoo pint. The flower spikes will not appear until April.

Nearer to me is a mixed flock of redwings and fieldfares. Compared with the plovers and gulls, these winter thrushes appear to have no legs as they search through the grass for food. The upright posture of the fieldfares and their jerky hops give them an angry look.

Two moorhens, not quite so dumpy as partridges and with longer legs, are searching for food about 30 metres from the ditch.

A stoat appears on the opposite side of the common. As it runs across the corner of the field the gulls take to the air. With them are the golden plover and lapwings. This is an opportunity to count them more accurately. There are fewer golden plover, recognisable by their narrower,

On the far side of the field are two birds. From their round shapes and small heads it is clear that they are partridges, but because they are against the light, it is impossible to see whether they have the horseshoe mark on the breast of the grey, or the pale throat and striped flanks of the red-legged.

Rob Hume

pointed wings—two, four, six, eight, ten, twenty, thirty, forty, fifty, two, three, four, five, six — fifty-six. Now for the lapwings — 160 approximately.

The redwings and fieldfares did not rise into the air like the plovers. They are still feeding. Instead, when the stoat appeared they took off as individuals, flying a short way out of danger and settling to feed again as quickly as possible. Apart from the thrushes the field seems empty of birds. A quick search shows that the partridges are no longer on the common and the moorhens have retreated to their ditch.

FOCUS on magpies

by Annette Preece

The bold, black and white plumage that makes the magpie such a well-known bird . . .

. . . can also break up its shape and make it difficult to see in a tree or bush.

Rob Hume

The whole truth

Some people do not like magpies because they eat eggs and young of other birds. But it is not really fair to pick on magpies. Many other creatures eat small birds too, for example grey squirrels, cats, jays, jackdaws and carrion crows. Also, studies of the magpie's diet show that only a tiny part of it, 3.5 per cent, consists of young birds. Most of their food is insects — including many which are harmful to us.

R Vaughan (Ardea)

Success story

Magpies are now doing very well in town gardens and parks. These may be similar to their favourite country areas — trees, hedges and scrub mixed with open ground for feeding. Country magpies are more timid because they are still shot in some areas. Town magpies are bolder and may even visit bird tables and sometimes steal milk or eggs left on doorsteps.

Enemies

Magpies also have their enemies. Grey squirrels and carrion crows will steal and eat magpie eggs and young. The domed roof of twigs on a magpie's nest is built to keep carrion crows out and nests built without a roof are often robbed. Carrion crows can also prevent magpies nesting by stealing their food and nests.

: C Wilkes (Aquila)

Guard birds

The Romans used to keep caged magpies outside their houses because their loud, machine-gun calls acted as a good burglar alarm. Magpies were also used as guard-dogs in poultry yards of English manor houses in the 14th century, to warn of approaching thieves.

Kept down

The bright, large magpie is an easy bird to see . . . and shoot. Last century they were wiped out in many areas where keepers wanted to protect their game birds from possible attack. Numbers were at their lowest early this century, then started to increase as gamekeepers became fewer. Strangely, in some areas of eastern England, numbers have fallen again since the 1950's. Reasons may include the removal of hedges and the use of pesticides by farmers.

M C Wilkes

what's in your

To help you identify the birds in your garden, here are some of the
most common ones you are likely to see in the winter, together
with a few unusual ones that may turn up.

Collared dove — pinky/grey
with black half-collar.
Monotonous three-note call. Less
common visitor.

Pied wagtail —
constantly walks and
wags tail. Less
common visitor

Mistle thrush —
bigger than song
thrush and greyer.
White outer tail
feathers show in flight.
Less common visitor.

Song thrush — warm
brown above, spotted
below. Alert looking.
Hops or runs.
Common.

Dunnock — creeps along
ground. Usually keeps close to
bushes. Fairly common.

Blackbird — male black, female
brown. Bold and common in
gardens.

garden?

Magpie — large black and white crow. Common in gardens in some areas.

Blackcap — greyish/brown, sparrow-sized bird. Male has black cap, female has brown cap. Unusual visitor.

Bullfinch — shy, plump bird with short, thick bill. White rump shows in flight. Fairly common.

Male

Redwing — white stripe over eye and under cheeks, red flanks. Less common winter visitor.

Female

Wren — secretive, tiny bird with upright tail. Sings in winter. Fairly common.

25

Sparrowhawk — fast-flying with broad, blunt wings. Collared dove size. Unusual visitor, swooping onto garden birds.

Starling — slightly smaller than a blackbird. Noisy and aggressive. Very common.

Robin — unmistakeable, visits most gardens.

Chaffinch — white on tail and wings in both sexes. Female duller than male. Common.

House sparrow — male is more colourful than female and has black bib. Noisy and common.

Blue tit — small and agile, found in most gardens.

Great tit — larger than blue tit. Black on head and belly. Common.

Male greenfinch — female is duller. Both have yellow on wings and tail, and thick bill. Common.

Male siskin
Small greeny/yellow birds with bright yellow wing bars. Female lacks black on head and is streakier. Unusual visitor.

Coal tit — white patch on back of head. Blue tit size.

Illustrations by Hilary Burn

27

MARCH

With the approach of spring, bird-watchers look forward with excitement to seeing their first spring migrants. When will the first summer visitor arrive? What species will it be? Will the swallows nest in the barn again? Thousands of people will be asking themselves the same questions. One of our earliest spring migrants is the blackcap, but take care, it could be winter visitor too! Keep a sharp eye open for early wild flowers, in woodland, in hedgerows and even your local churchyard.

LOOK AT Blackcaps

S & BA Craig (Aquila)

Key Facts

Scientific name: *Sylvia atricapilla*
Key features: great tit size. Grey-brown upperparts, pale grey underparts. Male's cap black; female's brown.
When seen: April to September, a few in winter.
Where seen: woodland with undergrowth, particularly brambles. Also tall hedges, shrubberies. Gardens in winter.
Nests: in thick vegetation.
Voice: short bursts of rich, warbling notes, from thick cover, sometimes from prominent perch. Heard early April-late June. Alarm call a sharp 'tack-tack'.
Food: insects, berries, or at bird tables.

If a blackcap turns up on your bird table this spring — it could be a winter visitor or a summer visitor!

Although blackcaps are mainly summer visitors, more and more are being seen in winter. But these wintering blackcaps are not the same birds that breed here. Some of them have been found wearing rings that were put on them in the breeding season in Austria, Germany and Switzerland. Perhaps when they migrate south in autumn, the mountain barrier of the Alps forces them north-west towards the British Isles.

In summer, blackcaps feed on insects among leaves, but they turn to berries as these ripen in autumn. Elder and yew berries are an important food for birds that are about to migrate, as well as for winter visiting blackcaps. In late winter they turn to ivy berries, which ripen in February, and some visit bird tables for food. In the winter of 1981/2 the British Trust for Ornithology found that blackcaps were visiting 21 per cent of bird tables in towns and 10 per cent in country areas.

Blackcaps may be confused with marsh or willow tits; they all have black caps, but the tits are smaller, rounder birds with shorter bills and browner plumage. Garden warblers are found in similar places and have songs very similar to blackcaps — but they sound less rich and varied, and have longer phrases.

Their powerful fluty songs have earned blackcaps the nickname mock nightingale. Because they collect grasses for their nests they are also known as jackstraws in Somerset and haybirds in Northamptonshire. Look out for blackcaps this spring. They are common in England and Wales where they may even breed in town parks with shrubberies. They are scarcer in Ireland and Wales.

nature
notebook

by Tim Cleeves

As I left the house on a clear and still March morning, two male blackbirds chased across the garden. One landed on a wall, drooped its wings and flicked up its long tail. On the bus ride to the reservoir, I could look down on the gardens below and see more blackbirds on songposts — corners of roofs, television aerials, washing-line posts. Each was defending its territory and occasionally chasing off intruders.

A pale yellow butterfly flew past — a brimstone, the first I had seen this year. Over 400 years ago, wildlife watchers called this beautiful insect a 'butter coloured fly'. A pair of black-headed gulls were bowing

At the reservoir, bright, spring flowers, coltsfoot and delicate, white wood anemones were growing near an old hawthorn hedge. Perhaps there had been a wood there once.

their heads towards each other, showing off their chocolate crowns and white 'eyebrows'. Soon these birds would probably be off to breed in the Welsh hills. Some black-headed gulls travel much further afield — many from Russia and eastern Europe move into midlands reservoirs in winter and leave in early spring.

With my telescope I could watch some goldeneyes on the reservoir. A pair were swimming together when another male approached them. Both males started to pump their heads up and down, eventually jerking them back and pointing their bills up in their display. Soon they would be migrating to nest and rear their young — perhaps in Finland or northern Sweden. They lay their eggs in natural nestholes in trees, or sometimes in special nestboxes put up for them by birdwatchers.

edge of a roof. It was sooty black, paler under the tail behind the dark legs; upright like a robin and with white flashes on the wings. It ran a little way along the roof edge, and, as it stopped, its tail quivered up and down — it was red! This was a male black redstart, a bird which breeds in very small numbers in the Midlands. Perhaps this newly arrived spring migrant was on its way to the city to seek out a nest site in a disused factory — a strange place for a rare bird, you might think, but just right for black redstarts!

Illustrated by David Thelwell

It was time for the bus, but I missed it! The reason was a flash of red disappearing over the railings near the pumping station. A bird popped up on the

FOCUS on churchyards
by Audrey Lincoln

A churchyard is often an oasis for wildlife. Grassland undisturbed for hundreds of years, old stone walls and very old trees provide excellent homes and food for a rich assortment of animals and plants.

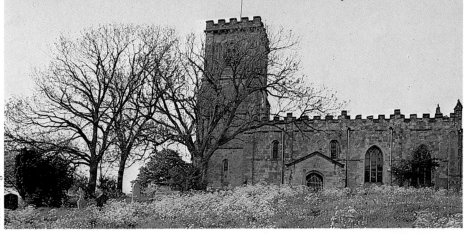

Heather Angel

Quiet visitors

Goldcrests and coal tits may be seen if there are conifers around the churchyard. The tiny goldcrest, Britain's smallest bird, searches for insects among the needles. Its nest is built towards the end of a branch, slung underneath like a hammock.

Heather Angel

Colourful cover

Gravestones may be hundreds of years old and many are covered in a patchwork of grey, green and orange lichens. Lichens are a fungus joined with an alga (a simple green plant) and have no roots. On all but the newest gravestones the bright orange *Xanthoria parietina* may be seen. It prefers to grow on gravestones where birds have perched and left their droppings, which provide extra food. Lichens grow very slowly, often only by 1 mm a year, but polluted air can prevent them from growing at all.

Grave hunter

The spotted flycatcher is often seen in churchyards. A small, brownish-grey bird that sits very upright, perches on the top of a gravestone, flits into the air, hovers, catches a fly and returns. A summer migrant, the spotted flycatcher winters in tropical and southern Africa and does not arrive in Britain until May. Its nest is placed against a wall, gravestone or tree trunk and is often hidden among vegetation, such as ivy.

Frank V Blackburn

Resting

On a warm, sunny day lizards may come out to sunbathe on tombstones or walls. Lizards are cold blooded and wait, motionless but alert, in the sun to increase their body temperature. They feed on spiders and insects, which are shaken until stunned and then swallowed.

Remains

Some churchyards may be the only areas of ancient pasture left in a village or town. When the grass has been undisturbed for hundreds of years it may still be a rich meadow with cowslips, orchids, ragged robin, daisies, clover and lots of other plants growing. In more shady, damp corners by gravestones and walls, **violets** and **primroses** may grow. In most churchyards, however, the grass is mown regularly, but in some it is not mown until mid July by which time the plants have flowered and set seed.

A survey of churchyards is being carried out by the Botanical Society of the British Isles (BSBI). They have already found that many shelter rare plants.

Heather Angel

33

Knock, knock

On some tombstones there may be a lot of broken snail shells. These have been left by a song thrush using the stone as an anvil. The thrush searches for snails among gravestones and along walls. Tiny snails may be eaten whole, but when it finds a large one it picks it up in its bill and flies or hops to the tombstone. Then it hammers the shell against the stone until broken and eats the soft snail inside.

S Downer (Aquila)

Fly-by-nights

At dusk the ghostly white shape of a **barn owl** floats across the churchyard and away to hunt for mice and voles. Barn owls are rarely seen in town, but in country areas they may roost or nest in church towers.

In city churchyards pipistrelle bats can be seen flying at dusk. Pipistrelles are our smallest and most common bat and often roost in churches. Bats feed on insects and in winter when these are scarce they hibernate in churches, hollow trees and caves.

Creepy plant

On walls bordering churchyards, or even on the church itself, a variety of plants may grow; yellow clumps of wallflowers, bright red valerian and tiny pale purple flowers of **ivy-leaved toadflax.** Ivy-leaved toadflax was introduced to Britain from the Mediterranean in the 17th century. The stems, which carry the seeds, turn away from light, so that the seeds will find cracks and crevices in the wall where they can germinate without being eaten by birds.

All-round favourite

Ivy growing up old trees or over church walls provides roost and nest sites for birds and is a source of food for many creatures. Ivy does not flower until the autumn, when it attracts red admirals and peacock butterflies in search of nectar. Because the berries ripen in early spring when those of other plants are over, they are eaten greedily by blackbirds and thrushes. The buds too are eaten — by second brood caterpillars of the holly blue butterfly. The first brood caterpillars feed on holly.

Thrush feast

From earliest times the yew tree has been planted in churchyards as a symbol of mourning. Its red berries ripen in September and are soon stripped by flocks of thrushes — first **blackbirds,** song and mistle thrushes, then fieldfares and **redwings** which arrive in Britain to spend the winter. Although birds such as nuthatches eat the hard seeds inside the berries, these are poisonous to people and other animals.

Cool customers

On cool, damp walls, ferns and mosses grow. The most common ferns are wall rue, male fern and **maidenhair spleenwort.** Ferns and most mosses cannot stand hot sun, but a few sorts of moss can be found growing in cushions along the wall top in full sun.

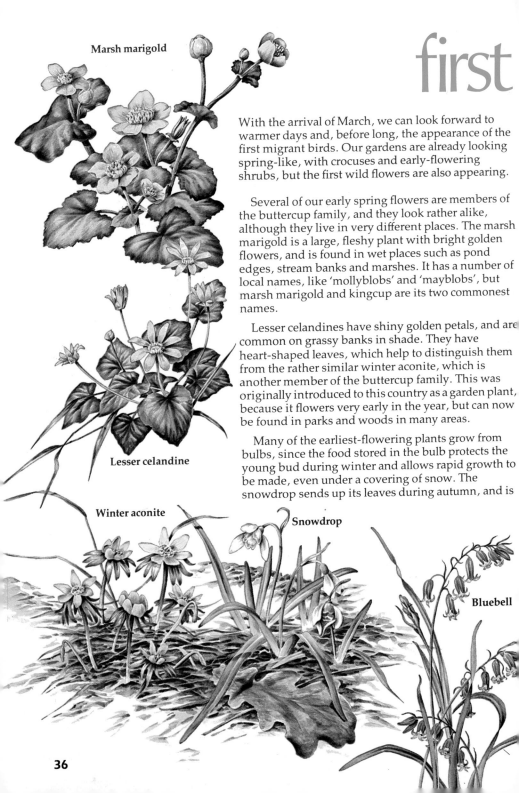

Marsh marigold

Lesser celandine

Winter aconite

Snowdrop

Bluebell

With the arrival of March, we can look forward to warmer days and, before long, the appearance of the first migrant birds. Our gardens are already looking spring-like, with crocuses and early-flowering shrubs, but the first wild flowers are also appearing.

Several of our early spring flowers are members of the buttercup family, and they look rather alike, although they live in very different places. The marsh marigold is a large, fleshy plant with bright golden flowers, and is found in wet places such as pond edges, stream banks and marshes. It has a number of local names, like 'mollyblobs' and 'mayblobs', but marsh marigold and kingcup are its two commonest names.

Lesser celandines have shiny golden petals, and are common on grassy banks in shade. They have heart-shaped leaves, which help to distinguish them from the rather similar winter aconite, which is another member of the buttercup family. This was originally introduced to this country as a garden plant, because it flowers very early in the year, but can now be found in parks and woods in many areas.

Many of the earliest-flowering plants grow from bulbs, since the food stored in the bulb protects the young bud during winter and allows rapid growth to be made, even under a covering of snow. The snowdrop sends up its leaves during autumn, and is

flowers

in flower by late winter (one of its country names is 'fair maids of February'). It grows in large colonies in woods and, like its relative the bluebell, its bulbs are a favourite winter food of badgers.

Woodland, because it offers shelter from the worst winter weather, is the home of many early spring flowering plants, some with large, showy flowers such as primroses and wood anemones. Others, like the moschatel, can be much more difficult to find. This plant has inconspicuous greenish flowers, which give it its other name of 'town hall clock', because the flower-head has four 'faces'.

Even patches of 'waste ground' such as disused railway lines or derelict land in city centres, can provide a home for spring flowers. One of the prettiest is coltsfoot, whose flowers, like small dandelions, push straight out of the ground, to be followed later by large roundish leaves with cobwebby surfaces. Closely related is the groundsel, a familiar weed which can be found in flower at any time of the year—this allows its seeds to take advantage of any newly-turned soil which might appear.

So next time you go for a walk, whether in the countryside or in your local park, keep a look-out for the flowers and plants too!

by Peter Newbery

Primrose

Wood anemone

Moschatel

Illustration by M Loates

Groundsel

Coltsfoot

37

APRIL

With the breeding season in full swing, April presents wonderful opportunities for watching bird behaviour. Everywhere there are birds singing, performing courtship flights or aggressive displays. Understanding what birds are doing puts a new angle on birdwatching. Don't be content with simply identifying a bird, learn about its behaviour too! As the trees come into full leaf you can learn to identify them as well and then discover what kinds of birds like to feed and nest in them.

LOOK AT
Yellowhammers

A T Moffett

Key Facts

Scientific name: *Emberiza citrinella*.
Key features: Male has yellow breast and head, brown back streaked with black; black tail with white outer-feathers; rusty rump. Females and juveniles duller but also have rust-coloured rumps.
Where seen: In winter on weedy fields. Farmland with hedges, heathland, young plantations.
Voice: *'Little-bit-of-bread-and-no-cheese'* song. Metallic *'chit'* call.
Food: Insects, worms, slugs and seeds.

The yellowhammer is quite a common bird, especially in areas of farmland where hedgerows are present, and on heathland, areas of scrub and young forestry plantations. The song is given from a high branch in a hedge or similar song post. It is used to show ownership of its territory and to attract a mate.

The nest is usually less than a metre above ground among rough vegetation or in a bush. The nest is a neat cup made of grasses and moss, lined with hairs. The eggs have a pale background, streaked with purple and black markings which give local names like 'the scribbler'.

In autumn and winter our native yellowhammers are joined by others from the continent. Flocks may number a hundred or more, sometimes mixed with reed and corn buntings, sparrows and finches. During winter they eat grain and weed seeds. By weighing yellowhammers as they fly to their communal roosts it has been shown that they know how cold it is going to be during the night. If it is going to be cold, yellowhammers eat more during the daytime, giving them extra energy to survive.

nature notebook

by Steve Rooke

The place is a wide, grassy footpath that runs between some large arable fields — about half a mile back from the sea on the east coast. Further inland is an area of low, rough ground which is nearly always flooded.

The weather is fine and clear with a light south-westerly wind. It is the last weekend in March.

Two species of bird are very evident. Lapwings are scattered over the fields in ones and twos, performing their hectic courtship flight, and calling loudly as they do so. High above them the weak sunshine has enticed a few skylarks into song. It takes me several minutes to locate the tiny dots in the sky that are the source of so much noise.

I walk on and suddenly there is a flash of white. A small bird skims low over the ground and up on to a fence post. It is a wheatear, a fine male and one of the birds I had hoped to see today.

Wheatears are often the first migrants to arrive back in this country and by sitting down and slowly scanning this field I find another two — one male and one female. They may stay near here to breed, but most continue to breeding areas on downs, moors, hilly pastures, cliffs and dunes further west.

Illustrations by Rob Hume

Behind them, further out in the field, three hares chase each other in circles over the dark earth. In the distance a small, isolated copse is alive with a swarm of rooks well into their breeding season

As soon as the flooded, low ground comes into view I stop and search the area through my binoculars. It is a very open spot and as a result difficult to watch without disturbing the birds.

There are three pied wagtails snapping at insects at the water's edge. But two of them are a very pale grey on the back and have no black joining the bib to the cap. This shows that they do not belong to our British race, but are probably on their way back to Scandinavia after spending winter in the Mediterranean.

A loud twittering announces another long distance migrant — a sand martin comes buzzing in over the water. It makes a few passes at some insects and then is gone, taking advantage of the fine weather to cover as much ground as possible.

FOCUS on aggression
by Annette Preece

Aggression (hostile behaviour) helps birds to survive by allowing them to drive away predators, and compete with their fellows for food, nesting and roosting sites and mates.

But pure attack is unusual — instead it is mixed with or replaced by displays that act as threats or scares without the need to fight...

Mute warning

The striking pose of this mute swan is meant to impress — but with its threat, not its beauty. The wings arched over the back and the drawn-in neck show that the swan is ready to attack if necessary. Mute swans are very aggressive in summer and will chase humans as well as birds from the large territory around their nest. Arguments over territory between males do not often turn into full scale fights. If they do it may be serious — nearly three per cent of ringed mute swans found dead are thought to have been killed in territorial fights.

K Hamar (Bruce Coleman Ltd)

Unruly mob

Owls and other predators are often mobbed by smaller birds or members of the crow family. This tawny owl is being mobbed at its daytime roost by a band of tits and goldcrests. They are making excited alarm calls to warn other birds of the owl's presence. This may also be a way of showing young birds which species are dangerous.

R A Hume

M G Hodgson

Pirates at large

Great skuas are fearsome pirates and spectacular acrobats, chasing gulls, terns, gannets and even herons to steal the food from them. They force their victims to disgorge or drop their catch by striking them with their powerful bills and feet or grabbing their tails or wings and tumbling them. The scientific name for this pirates' way of feeding is kleptoparasitism (from the Greek *kleptein*, to steal; and parasite, one that lives at the expense of others.)

S Jonasson (Frank W Lane)

Beware!

Fulmars will spurt a horrible-smelling oil at human and other intruders who go too near their nests. The first attempts to re-introduce the white-tailed eagle as a breeding species — in Fair Isle — failed because of fulmars oiling the eagles! Mute swans, merlins, kestrels, owls, skuas, gulls and terns will also attack people in the breeding season.

T Andrewartha (Ardea)

Song and dance

By the end of March oystercatchers have established and are defending a small territory around the nest scrape and frightening away intruders by 'piping' displays. With their heads down and bills open the pair run to and fro making a shrill piping noise. Like most threat displays this is usually enough to drive off any intruders — but if not, then fierce fighting may follow.

R A Hume

Quarrelling coot

Coots are very quarrelsome birds and may fight even in winter when they are not defending a breeding territory. Fights where two birds rush at each other then rise up and beat the water with both feet and wings add a spectacular touch to winter birdwatching.

Sing out a warning

Song contains a mixture of messages. A blackbird singing on a bright morning in spring is, in effect, saying to other birds of its kind 'I am a male blackbird. This is my territory. Other males should keep out, but females may enter!'

So it is both a long distance warning to other male birds to keep away and an invitation to females. By advertising his ownership of a territory in this way a male bird avoids confusion and fighting — and keeps an area where it can mate and nest safely and find enough food.

Eric Hosking

Moving message

Where birds of a species nest close together there is no need for a long distance warning song, and a variety of antics may be used to advertise their small territory and so keep other individuals out of the area. Black-headed gulls use their dark hoods as a warning signal —

emphasising it in the forward threat posture seen on the left.

However, a breeding pair show their lack of aggression to each other with a head flagging display where the threatening black hood is deliberately turned away from the mate.

Ordered pecks

Fighting for food often breaks out in winter when birds are hungry and food is short. Tits will chase off and steal food from each other on bird feeders and tables. There is a 'peck order' among them — great tit is at the top of the list, followed by blue tit, marsh tit

and coal tit. The great tit is at the top of the list because it is the bird that usually beats the others, the next in the list usually defeats the ones below but not the ones above and so on. However, this is not strict and very aggressive blue tits may chase off great tits.

WHAT'S THAT TREE ?

You can identify trees from shape, fruit and flowers, colour and texture of bark or by leaf shape.

Here are some of our most common trees with hints on how to recognise them at this time of year.

Beech

Smooth, grey bark. Leaves lower than two metres stay on in winter. Each spiny husk splits open to release two triangular, brown nuts — favourite food of tits and finches. Leaves cast dense shade and so few green plants grow below it.

Pedunculate oak

May live for 800 years. Lobed leaves and acorns on long stalks. Deeply creviced, grey bark may be covered in lichen if air is unpolluted. On dry soils and steep slopes in the west, the sessile oak with its rounded, stalkless acorns, is more common.

English elm

Told from a distance by its shape — in summer has a billowing, 'thundercloud' look. Leaves have a rough, hairy surface.

Common ash

Told even in winter by black buds and smooth grey bark on twigs and young trunks. Compound leaf, ie, a number of leaflets along a central stalk. Bunches of seeds are known as keys. Prefers damp, lime-rich soil.

Silver birch

Silver white, paper bark. Slender trunk and small, toothed leaves. Male catkins are brown and upright in autumn — they become longer and hang down in spring. Fruit is green/brown and sausage-shaped. Tiny seeds are eaten by siskins and redpolls.

Alder

Grows near water. Leaves blunt edged and toothed. Small, brown cones shed small seeds in autumn — fed on by siskins and redpolls. Bark is dark grey to nearly black.

Scots pine

Grows wild in the Scottish highlands, but now widely planted by man. Pointed shape when young but flat-topped when older. Blue/green needles grow in pairs and stay on in winter. Scaly plates of brown or red bark flake off the trunk.

Norman Arlott 80.

MAY

The warm days of late spring throb to the soft, soothing, purring call of the turtle dove. This delicate member of the pigeon family is one of the last summer migrants to arrive. Another common sound in May is the monotonous call of the cuckoo. You may even be lucky enough to see a young cuckoo being fed by a foster parent much smaller than itself. At this time of year it is quite common to find young birds looking lost and abandoned, but a parent is almost always nearby waiting for you to go away! So the message is 'leave young birds alone'!

LOOK AT turtle doves

Now is the time to listen for the soothing 'turrr turrr' call that gives the turtle dove its name. For this, the most delicate looking of our doves and pigeons, is the only one that is a summer migrant, deserting us again in September to fly south of the Sahara desert.

E A Janes (Aquila)

Pairs of turtle doves sitting on telegraph wires are a common sight over much of England in summer. Their black and white tails are very eyecatching as they fly away. But don't look for them in towns or uplands, for they are mainly birds of low farmland and open woodland.

In fact, their distribution is remarkably similar to that of a pretty weed called fumitory. This is common on cultivated or disturbed ground. Although turtle doves eat the shoots and seeds of many plants, up to half their diet may consist of fumitory seeds alone.

In late July and August, adult turtle doves desert any remaining eggs and young in the nest. This cut-off in breeding activity is necessary to give adults and fledged young enough time to build up reserves of body fat and moult their flight feathers before they migrate. Most pairs, however, manage to raise at least two broods of young in a season.

Like other pigeons and doves, but unlike most birds, turtle doves can suck up water and so do not need to tilt back their heads when drinking.

Key Facts

Scientific name: *Streptopelia turtur*
Key features: chestnut back, black and white tail. 28 cm long.
When seen: late April to September (a few in October).
Where seen: farmland and open woodland. Uncommon in Scotland, Ireland and north and west of England and Wales.
Nests: platform of twigs in tree or hedge.
Food: seeds and shoots.
Voice: a repeated, purring 'turrr turrr'.

nature notebook

by Annette Preece

On a May morning in my small, town garden the blackbird's rich notes blend with the wheeze of a greenfinch and the spluttering wren's song. In the background a great tit sings 'tee-chu, tee-chu', sparrows chirp and starlings imitate them all.

In the evening, blackbirds are still singing and chasing each other off their territories. A song thrush sings higher up, from the top of the apple tree. One evening last May it sang until 10 pm — at least an hour after sunset.

Interesting weeds are now springing up on the lawn. Daisies, dandelions, lilac ivy-leaved speedwell and small-flowered cranesbill are flowering. Buttercups will flower later and their seeds, together with dandelion clocks, may attract bullfinches to feed.

While preparing my vegetable bed I keep digging up shiny, brown moth pupae. I cover them up again so that they can turn into winged adults when they are ready. They will become one of the 300 species of moth in the Noctuid family.

its wings. From June these and other attractive moths fly into the house, and their large numbers attract small bats to my garden.

One of the commonest Noctuid moths is the large yellow underwing. At rest its dull, brown forewings camouflage it. But when disturbed it flies off, flashing bright yellow under

Lots of broken snail shells suddenly appear on the path. Song thrushes are making the most of the snails' awakening after winter. Snails and slugs festoon the flowerbeds at night and two other garden dwellers, recently woken from winter sleep, are also enjoying the feast — hedgehogs and toads.

FOCUS on moorhens

by Irene Allen

Wherever there is fresh water, you will probably see a moorhen — but these shy birds are equally at home on land.

Roger Wilmshurst

Worldspread

Moorhens are common over most of the British Isles — except in very high areas where the only water is fast-flowing, or there is no cover for them to skulk in. They like any still or slow-moving water, from small ditches to lakes, and are found in every continent of the world except Australia. Moorhens belong to the same family as coots, water rails and corncrakes.

Big feet

Although moorhens look very clumsy, their big feet allow them, not only to walk and run quickly, but to swim, perch and climb trees as well! Also their long toes help to spread their weight so that they do not sink on soft mud or floating vegetation. Coots, which spend more time on water, have fleshy lobes on the sides of their toes to help them swim and dive.

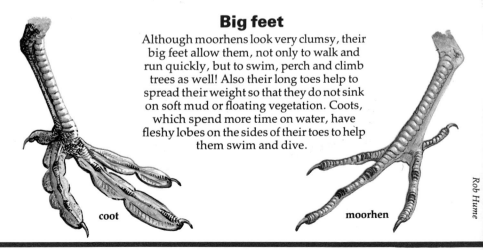

coot

moorhen

Rob Hume

High rise nests

Moorhens usually nest quite low down, among the bankside vegetation or on a low branch hanging over the water. But nests have been found up to eight metres high in bushes and trees — sometimes in old nests of magpies or woodpigeons. Floating nests are built on a platform of twigs and those in water deeper than 20 cm usually have a ramp leading up to them, making it easier for the birds to climb up.

F Gohier (Ardea)

Hold tight

When danger approaches, moorhens often dive underwater and grasp a piece of weed with their feet to hold themselves under. The only part that shows above water is the tip of the bill which acts as a snorkel.

Nests for all occasions

In early spring before building a cup-shaped nest for egg-laying, moorhens often build a platform of piled-up vegetation on which they can display to each other. Once the eggs in the true nest have hatched, the parents may build another 'brood' nest for the young to use. For a second brood, they either build yet another nest, or improve the first one.

G Ziesler (Bruce Coleman)

Redheads

When they hatch, baby moorhens have a bare red patch on their heads and depend on their parents for food for about three weeks. They beg for food by moving their tiny, stumpy wings in a rowing action and pushing their red heads upwards, which stimulates their parents to feed them. As they become more able to feed themselves, the red fades.

Spring fever

In the breeding season pairs of moorhens defend a territory for feeding and nesting and are quite aggressive. They may chase off their own young once they are fully grown, but sometimes young of the first brood may look after the young of later broods. In autumn and winter adults are much less aggressive and chicks born late in the season may be allowed to stay with their parents until the next spring. When two pairs of moorhens fight, the two males and the two females usually fight each other.

M C Wilkes (Aquila)

Showing the colours

The moorhen's red shield is used as a threat to other birds. In winter flocks some birds dominate others. These dominant birds are not the largest in size but those with the largest shield. In courtship the head is lowered to hide the shield.

White patches under the tail are also used in displays. The tail is fanned out to show them off to intruders in a 'hunched display'. When courting a female the male will swim round her with his tail raised to display his white patches.

Rob Hume

M C Wilkes

Right from the start

Coots and moorhens look rather similar at first glance. But coots are larger, rounder birds with white bills and face shields. Moorhens flick their tails which shows off the white feathers underneath. Coots are birds of open, deep water, while moorhens prefer the plant-covered edges or ditches.

All sorts

Moorhens feed while swimming or walking and will sometimes snatch food from other birds such as great crested grebes. They eat all sorts of things including spiders, earthworms, crab apples, pondweed leaves and stems, tadpoles and buttercup seeds.

Merely moorhens

It seems strange that a bird that spends all its time on or near water should be called a moorhen. The old name of waterhen seems much better. In fact it used to be called a merehen; mere is the word for a lake or pool, but the way people said it slowly changed until it became moorhen.

M Hodgson

DIPPING IN

Birds that flock together at some times of year may also enjoy a communal bath — sparrows, starlings and blue tits are examples. Other more solitary species, like this **song thrush**, drive off other birds that come too close.

Most birds drink by taking water in their beaks and then tilting back their heads to let the water trickle down their throats. But **woodpigeons** like other pigeons, doves and some gamebirds can suck up water continuously.

Summer is here and should there be any hot, dry spells the sight of water will be more attractive than usual to birds.

Birds need water all year round for drinking and bathing. Make a bird bath or pond in your garden where you can watch it from the house and get better views of birds like this **house sparrow.**

January is another time of year when garden ponds and bird baths are very important. In frosty weather they may be the only ice-free water for birds such as this **brambling** — a winter visitor.

57

JUNE

The hum and buzz of insects on a hot, summer's day is a reminder to look for birds feeding in the air. Swifts, swallows and martins all catch insects in flight, but keep an eye open for broods of young spotted flycatchers, sparrows, starlings and even black-headed gulls feeding in this way. If you are lucky enough to live in an area where nightjars are still found, try to persuade your parents or YOC leaders to take you birdwatching at dusk on a warm evening. Watching these nocturnal birds hawking silently for moths turns birdwatching into a real adventure!

LOOK AT
spotted
flycatchers

If you visit a park or large garden this month you stand a good chance of seeing a small brown bird dart out of cover then, equally quickly, turn in mid-air and dash back. In fact, July seems to be the easiest time to see spotted flycatchers, because all the young of the first broods have left their nests.

E A Janes

A spotted flycatcher's striking behaviour makes up for its rather plain appearance. Sitting very upright on a perch, it flicks its wings and tail, then suddenly darts out after a flying insect, hovering for an instant, then twisting in mid-air and landing back on its perch. Bristles at the side of its bill help to make a wider net for catching insects.

When the young first hatch, they can only eat small insects, so the parent flycatchers have to catch large numbers of these to make up the bulk. As the young grow, they can eat larger and larger insects which are easier for the parents to catch. Spotted flycatchers hunt all sorts of aerial insects, including butterflies; and they can tell wasps and bees from similar but harmless hoverflies — carefully removing the stings from the former.

June and July are the peak times for flying insects and this is when spotted flycatchers breed. They cannot stay here in winter as their food is scarce, so they fly to tropical Africa after breeding — not to return until the following May.

Key facts

Scientific name: *Muscicapa striata*
Key features: upright stance, large eye. Soft grey above, pale streaked below.
When seen: late May to September (migration starts in late July).
Where seen: woodland edges, parks, gardens, even in city centres.
Nests: against wall or tree trunk, sometimes in holes. Will use open-fronted nestboxes.
Food: flying insects, sometimes ground insects.
Voice: thin, high-pitched 'zeet'.

nature notebook

by Chris Harbard

In June the songs of our resident birds are joined by those of summer visitors to our country. The dawn chorus of wrens, robins and blackbirds is joined by willow warblers, redstarts and

blackcaps, while the normal quiet of dusk is broken by nightjars, grasshopper warblers and, in some places, nightingales.

Many of our summer visitors eat insects and arrive here to find insect life becoming plentiful once more. Hibernating queen bees emerge and produce broods of workers that are busy foraging for food. Look for large and small white butterflies which will be laying their eggs. You may also see an orange-tip.

The hawthorn, may still be in bloom, its white flowers adding variety to the countryside and its strong scent attracting many insects. The greenfinch is now nesting in the hedges, from which the rattling song of the lesser whitethroat can sometimes be heard.

The sudden abundance of natural food comes at the same time as the nestlings of resident birds such as song thrushes, blue tits, chaffinches and robins. This is a busy time of year for parent birds. They spend the daylight hours continually searching for food to satisfy their hungry young.

Swifts have returned from Africa to scream, high in the sky, feeding with swallows and martins. Sedge warblers announce their presence from riverside bushes and in nearby fields, yellow wagtails feed amongst the cows. Spotted flycatchers dart out to catch their food from the woodland edges, and the female cuckoo gives her bubbling call as she searches for a suitable nest in which to lay her eggs.

Illustrations by Alan Harris

FOCUS on gardens

by Annette Preece

In Britain 80% of homes have gardens — from a flower bed by the front door to the parkland of a country estate. Each is home for all sorts of animals and plants — a nature reserve on the doorstep! So what's in a garden for birds?

J Robinson (BNHP)

Creepy crawlies

Underneath the calm surface of a compost heap is a mine of activity — small insects, spiders, fungi and bacteria busy feeding on the plant matter and speeding up the process of decay. In winter a compost heap provides a frost-free area where birds can find food.

Garden nurseries

You can encourage more birds to live in your garden by providing plenty of places to nest. One way to do this is to put up nestboxes — on the walls, fences or trees. These can be bought from the RSPB — or you can make one yourself. Different sorts of nestbox are available which will attract different birds.

Try to put your nestbox in a quiet part of the garden and where cats cannot easily reach it (eg not at the top of a wall).

You could also put an old jug, kettle or tea pot (spout down to keep out rain) in a tree or shrub. Robins are well known for using these unusual nest sites.

D Washington (?)

Stephen Dalton (NHPA)

Invaders!

Blackbirds were originally woodland birds and it was not until the 1830's that they were first noticed in gardens in winter. Then they spread into the centre of our towns and are now commoner in town gardens than in countryside. One reason for this may be that the blackbird is very adventurous in its diet, unlike its relative the song thrush, and has quickly learnt to use any food it can find in gardens. In fact, blackbirds outnumber song thrushes by about 20 to 1 in gardens.

Spare the weeds!

Most of us have been taught from an early age that weeds are 'a bad thing'. But many are both beautiful and important food for insects and birds. Some, like chickweed and groundsel, flower all through the winter when other natural food is scarce.

See if you can leave a clump of nettles to grow in an otherwise unused, dark corner — along a hedge or behind a garden shed. Butterflies that lay their eggs on nettles include red admirals, peacocks and small tortoiseshells. Moth caterpillars also feed on nettles — and many of them will in turn be eaten by the birds in your garden.

E A Janes

Facts and figures

One hundred and ten different sorts of birds are known to visit gardens for food in winter. But you are more likely to see between five and 50 different species — depending on where you live.

Bird table top twelve

1. House sparrow
2. Starling
3. Blue tit
4. Chaffinch
5. Blackbird
6. Greenfinch
7. Great tit
8. Dunnock
9. Robin
10. Collared dove
11. Coal tit
12. Song thrush

Going for a song

When a song thrush feeds on the lawn, cocking its head on one side to watch or listen for any trace of movement, it is not searching for earthworms alone. Among the blades of grass and in the soil are hundreds and thousands of tiny creatures — snails, centipedes, slugs, spiders, beetles, ants and earwigs, to name a few.

E A Janes

Plant a tree

Willows are trees rich in insect life —
250 species of insect have been found
living among their leaves and
branches. In autumn alder seeds are a
favourite food of siskins, redpolls and
other finches. Other deciduous trees
harbour vast numbers of insects —
oak is by far the best with an average
of 300 species; silver birch has 225
and poplar 100. Berry-bearing trees
and shrubs such as berberis,
cotoneaster, rowan and hawthorn will
also attract birds to your garden in
winter.

Ivy

Ivy is many things to many different
animals. Dunnocks, chaffinches and
blackbirds nest safely hidden among the
twining stems. The evergreen leaves
provide all-year shelter from rain and cold
and insect food for small mammals and
birds; while berries are a valuable source
of food in late winter when other supplies
are running out. Adult peacock and
tortoiseshell butterflies may hibernate in
ivy for the winter.

Old timers

Ringing records can tell us how long birds live. Most die young but some birds have survived over 30 years, including an oystercatcher and a curlew. Also, in the Antarctic there are several royal albatross adults ringed over 40 years ago. But, no wild birds can beat the all-time record, a sulphur-crested cockatoo at London Zoo over 80 years old!

Flight to nowhere

The effect of cold weather was clearly shown by a redwing during the freezing cold January of 1963. The bird was ringed in a garden in Nuneaton, Warwickshire on 4 January. Three days later it was found dead on a boat in the mid-Atlantic almost 2,500 kms away! The boat was going eastwards towards Ireland and so had not carried the bird across. The redwing must have 'missed' Ireland and kept going.

Return a ring

The address on a bird ring is very important as it allows the finder to report the bird to the people who ringed it. British rings have either BTO TRING ENGLAND or BRIT MUSEUM LONDON SW7. Someone who did not know about ringing, found a dunnock in Lincolnshire, and wrote to report that the bird must have escaped from the museum in London before they had time to stuff it!

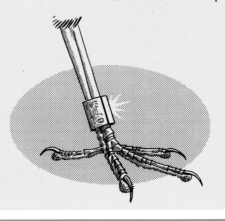

Non-stop swifts

Some old birds must have flown astonishing distances. The oldest British-ringed swift is over 16 years old. Since swifts are in flight all the time, except for the short time on the nest in summer, this bird has probably flown over eight million kilometres. This is the same as ten return trips to the moon or 100 days in Concorde at full speed — all achieved by a bird weighing about 40 g.

Knot so fast!

The fast recovery of a young knot has given us an idea of the speed of migration of some waders. It was ringed on the Wash (east England) on 3 September then reported from the Bomi Hills of Liberia (west Africa) 5,200 kms away, eight days later. The bird must have flown an average of 650 kms each day.

Worldwide bird

One of most travelled species from Britain is the Manx shearwater. Every winter some ringed birds are found in the South Atlantic off Brazil, Uruguay or Argentina and there are often one or two records of young birds in eastern North American waters. The first record of a British-ringed bird in Australia was also a Manx shearwater. Ringed on Skokholm (off South Wales) as a nestling, it was found 14 months later in South Australia.

M Hodgson

JULY

The long summer holiday is a great time for birdwatching. There is always plenty to do. The long days give you time to go out and discover new things close to home, even if you are not going away on holiday. Why not try to get a few of your school friends interested in birds if they are complaining that there is nothing to do?

Why not keep a special holiday diary? You can then enjoy looking back on your summer birdwatching even in the middle of next winter!

LOOK AT

OYSTERCATCHERS

Key Facts

Scientific name: *Haemotopus ostralegus.*
Key features: Large, black and white wader with long bright orange beak and pink legs. Very noisy. In winter adults have a white collar.
Where seen: mainly on seashore and estuaries in summer and winter.
Nest: Small scrape on ground which may be lined with vegetation or small stones.
Voice: Shrill piping trill; loud *'pic, pic, pic'.*
Food: Shellfish, especially mussels, cockles and limpets; worms, insects and crustaceans.

Oystercatchers are eye-catching waders which are seen throughout the year on our coasts and estuaries. They breed on the coast around Britain but in northern England and Scotland they also breed inland along river valleys. The 2-4 eggs are laid normally in May. Both parents incubate the eggs; the young leave the nest when about 12 hours old and fly after 5 weeks.

Oystercatchers are normally seen on the edge of water or mud probing for food or roosting at high tide in huge flocks. They can, however, swim well and may even land on the water and rest. Oystercatchers are often active and noisy at night.

The oystercatcher's long, powerful, orange bill is used to open shellfish such as mussels and cockles. They use two different feeding methods to remove the soft body of the shellfish from its hard shell. Some oystercatchers stab the muscle which keeps the shell closed and their beaks have pointed tips. Other oystercatchers hammer the shells open; their beaks have blunt tips. Young oystercatchers, unlike most waders, are fed by their parents.

From late February to late July oystercatchers can be seen performing their piping display, in which pairs with their beaks pointing downward, either facing each other or side by side, call loudly together.

Oystercatchers do not breed until the females are four years old and the males five. They are long-lived birds with many living for over 20 years. A German one lived for 34 years!

nature notebook

by John Andrews

When it's really hot, nobody wants to do anything and even the cat comes indoors to lie in the shade. That's the time to head for the nearest pond.

It's cooler by the water and there's plenty going on. Dragonflies hunt up and down, sometimes chasing each other, like tiny fighter planes. The small blue or red damselflies flutter close to the bank — you can get right up to them, but the bigger dragonflies are wary and are best watched through binoculars.

Binoculars are useful for fish-watching too. Where the surface is shaded, and there are no reflections, you can see big fish basking lazily in the warmth. Red fins mean roach or rudd, striped flanks are perch.

Alan Harris

70

Look out for pike — lean and mean, they lurk in the weeds, ever ready to pounce on other fish or swirl to the surface to pull down a luckless duckling. Close to the bank there may be sticklebacks, the males beautifully red and bronze-green, as aggressive and handsome as dragonflies.

Every pond attracts birds, if only a pair of moorhens skulking in the reeds. Swallows and martins compete with the dragonflies to catch gnats and sometimes scoop up a drink in flight, or deliberately splash into the water to take a flying bath. If you're lucky, you might even see a hobby. These agile falcons often visit ponds to hunt swallows — and dragonflies too. When a hobby catches a big dragonfly, it holds it in one foot and eats it like a crunchy ice cream cornet as it flies along!

As evening comes, the gnats really swarm — great clouds of them dancing above the water. Many kinds don't bite people but enough do: soon you'll be scratching, and then it's high time to go home!

FOCUS on herring gulls
by Irene Allen

The herring gull is probably the second most numerous gull in Britain. In a full survey of Britain's breeding seabirds, Operation Seafarer in 1969-70, 300,000 pairs were breeding in coastal areas. Most numerous was the kittiwake with 470,000 pairs.

Anything goes

Herring gulls do not, as their name suggests, feed only on fish, although they often follow fishing boats or scavenge fishing ports for waste fish. They also eat small mammals, such as moles and young rabbits, carrion, chicks and eggs stolen from their own or other species, and food pickings from rubbish tips.

Land lubbers

Herring gulls are no longer just seabirds. Although colonies are usually on cliffs or low-lying coastal areas, in the 1920's they started nesting on buildings on the south coast and now breed inland.

Cannibals

Parent herring gulls take great care not to both be away from the nest at once. Eggs or chicks left unguarded in a colony are likely to be eaten by neighbours or other predators, such as foxes. Gulls will also attack eggs and young of other species nesting in the open, such as lapwings, oystercatchers, eiders, and young shelducks.

Take cover

Chicks and eggs have brownish grey, speckled colouring which gives them camouflage against predators. Very young chicks crouch and stay still to blend into the background if an alarm is raised. Older chicks run to a hideaway and then crouch.

Smashing!

Hard food such as shellfish is cracked by dropping it from a great height. This often takes several tries because herring gulls do not seem to realise that objects dropped on hard rocks break more quickly than those dropped on soft sand, mud or water! They have been seen repeatedly dropping shells into sand when an ideal, hard rock was nearby!

R T Mills

Dennis Green (Bruce Coleman Ltd)

Day...

A summer day, and the edge of a wood is bustling with activity. Small birds search through the undergrowth for insects, snails and seeds, while a kestrel watches closely for a possible victim. Butterflies look for bramble and campion flowers to feed on, while caterpillars eat their favourite plants or are eaten by chaffinches. A stoat has just pounced on a bank vole, but the robin continues to sing uninterrupted. . . .

1. Swifts 2. Swallows 3. Kestrel 4. Tawny owl 5. Robin 6. Brimstone butterfly 7. Buff tip moth caterpillar 8. Magpie 9. Blackbird 10. Stoat 11. Garden chafer 12. Small tortoiseshell butterfly 13. Chaffinch 14. Common field grasshopper 15. Bindweed 16. Ladybirds 17. Wren 18. Red and white campion.

...Night

Darkness, and most of the creatures you saw in the day have hidden. But far from being still, the wood is alive with a new set of creatures. Scented white campion and honeysuckle attract night flying moths and nocturnal caterpillars feed on the oak leaves. A badger eats the remains of the dead rabbit, while a woodcock searches for worms.

Where the kestrel was perched, a tawny owl waits and listens for a mouse or vole. The faint rustlings of the wood are interrupted only by the nightingale's song. . . .

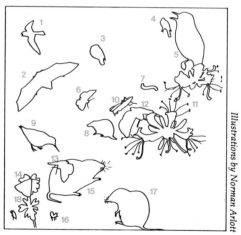

Illustrations by Norman Arlott

1. Nightjar 2. Pipistrelle bat 3. Tawny owl
4. Kestrel 5. Nightingale 6. Red underwing moth
7. Common lutestring moth caterpillar 8. Badger
9. Woodcock 10. Great green bush cricket
11. Honeysuckle 12. Death's head hawkmoth
13. Magpie moth 14. Silver Y moth 15. Bank vole
16. Glow worms 17. Shrew 18. Red and white campion.

AUGUST

August is a quiet month in terms of birdsong. Most songbirds no longer need to hold territory and become rather secretive as they moult their feathers and grow new ones. At the end of the breeding season you will notice some birds, such as blackbirds, looking very ragged. Mallards and other ducks go through a brief flightless period because they lose their flight feathers all at once. During this period the males become rather dull and look very like the females. Keep a sharp eye open for young birds which have not yet moulted into adult plumage; young robins, greenfinches and bullfinches can all look very odd!

LOOK AT
Yellow wagtails

Roger Wilmshurst (Bruce Coleman)

Key Facts

Scientific name: *Motacilla flava*
Key features: smaller than pied wagtail, bright yellow underparts in spring.
Where seen: wet meadows and marshes mainly in England and Wales.
When seen: summer.
Voice: sweet-sounding 'tsweep'.
Food: insects.

August is the time when families of yellow wagtails gather into feeding flocks. They are slim birds with long tails and canary-yellow underparts. Males are brighter than females and have yellow heads.

Like other wagtails they walk or run with their tails wagging up and down as they snatch small insects from the grass. Sometimes they flutter into the air to seize their prey. They regularly call as they fly with a typically bouncy flight.

One of the best places to look for yellow wagtails is near cattle and horses; the birds keep close to the animals' feet where they can snatch any insects which are disturbed.

Yellow wagtails spend the winter in tropical Africa and the first migrants may return to Britain as early as March, but most arrive in April. Different races return to separate parts of Europe: our race with its yellow head is rare outside Britain; while the blue-headed race which breeds in western Europe may sometimes be seen here. If you visit other parts of Europe this summer you may spot yellow wagtails with blue, grey or even black heads.

Although very common in some parts of Britain there are large areas where yellow wagtails do not breed and they are scarce in the West Country, western Wales and Scotland. In future these attractive migrants may lose some of their breeding places as wet meadows are drained and ponds and other wet areas are filled in.

nature notebook

by Peter Holden

Two black eyes peer from the bottom of a hedge where harebells and white campion sway gently in the breeze. Nearby, two young rabbits nibble the short turf. Suddenly, a long, slim stoat bounds from cover; the rabbits panic and bolt down the nearest burrow. The stoat has failed this time to catch its meal, but will try again elsewhere. Brambles in the hedge make safe places for many small birds to nest, including blackcaps, garden warblers and whitethroats. Long-tailed tits nested there earlier in the year and the soft, domed nest is now deserted. Family groups of these attractive birds travel along the hedgerows keeping in contact with their squeaking calls and hoarse trills. Soon these groups will join together to form even larger flocks.

Bramble flowers attract many butterflies, the most numerous being gatekeepers and meadow browns. The caterpillars of these two butterflies feed on grasses, but the adults like the bramble's sweet nectar. They also help the plant by transferring some of its pollen on their heads or mouth-parts.
On river banks, drake mallards

August and September they will moult again and slowly re-grow their bright breeding plumage. As evening approaches, parties of

swim among the reeds in the water's edge. They have moulted into their dull eclipse plumage and look like females except for their bills that stay yellow-green. Some have lost their flight feathers and their dull plumage helps to hide them at this dangerous time. In

swifts scream over towns and villages. Young swifts are flying with the adults and all are busy feeding in preparation for their migratory flight to Africa. Suddenly, one day in late August, they will disappear leaving the evening sky strangely quiet.

Illustrations by Norman Arlott

focus on WADERS

by Peter Holden

'Wader' is the name used to describe plovers, sandpipers and their close relatives. Most waders are regularly found near open water or in marshy places. In North America they are called 'shorebirds'.

Dennis Green

R Tidman (Bruce Coleman)

Inland moves

Although many waders spend most of the year near the coast, some species, like curlew or this **greenshank**, may nest inland miles away from the sea. Dunlins also leave their usual coastal beaches and estuaries in spring and move to moorland to nest.

Not what they seem

If the male and female of a species are different in appearance, it is usually the male that is the more colourful of the pair. Two British waders are exceptions to this rule, the **dotterel** and the red-necked phalarope. In both cases the females are more brightly coloured and attract a mate by display flights; the males carry out much of the incubation and care for the young.

On the level

Waders are at home on the ground and that is where most of them lay their eggs. **Green sandpipers**, however, lay their eggs in the old nests of other birds, especially thrushes, which have been built in trees.

Bendy bills

Many waders look for their food in mud or soft earth, but how do they find their prey without seeing it, and how do they pull it to the surface?

The tip of a wader's bill is very sensitive and locates food by touch. It is also surprisingly pliable, allowing the bird to open the tip of its bill without opening the whole length. You can see this in the **woodcock** shown here. To discover how important this is, try pushing a pair of tweezers into soil and then opening them!

One-parent families

Not all wader families stay together for the breeding season. Female **redshanks** often move to another area before the chicks are fully grown, leaving the male to look after them. This habit may help the young to survive when there is a shortage of food: the young feed themselves and an extra adult would only use up more food.

J B & S Bottomley

E Soothill (Aquila)

A J Bond (Aquila)

83

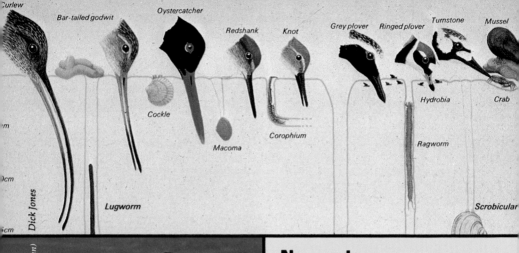

Curlew
Bar-tailed godwit
Oystercatcher
Redshank
Knot
Grey plover
Ringed plover
Turnstone
Mussel
Cockle
Macoma
Corophium
Hydrobia
Crab
Ragworm
Lugworm
Scrobicular
Dick Jones
m
)cm
cm

L Lee Rue (Bruce Coleman)

Roger Tidman

No overlap

All these waders have bills of different lengths which means that they can reach to various depths and discover different foods.

Legs and feet

Waders' feet are well adapted to life on the ground. The hind toe that allows perching birds to grip is tiny or has disappeared completely. **Avocets**, which live in very wet conditions and swim regularly, have webs between the toes, while phalaropes have partly webbed feet for swimming and stirring up food in shallow pools.

Long-legged waders, such as redshanks and godwits, are able to walk into the water, while shorter-legged species like turnstones cannot usually venture beyond the mud or shallows.

Bills

Godwits, curlews and snipes have long bills for probing. Avocets use their delicate, upturned bills to sweep from side to side and filter tiny animals out of shallow water. Turnstones use their short, stout bills for turning small stones or seaweed to find crabs and other creatures hidden below. **Oystercatchers** either open mussels with blows from their powerful bills, or carefully prize open the shell if a gap can be found.

Roving young

Wader chicks are covered in down when they hatch and they can move about quickly and leave their nests. They are very different from many other birds whose young are blind, naked and helpless for many days after hatching.

The mobility of this young **oystercatcher**, together with its excellent camouflage, gives it better protection from enemies such as foxes, stoats, crows, gulls and birds of prey.

Keep moving

Many waders migrate across whole continents — some sanderlings which breed north of the Arctic Circle spend winter in South Africa. Golden plovers also migrate, but their movements are usually from high moorland where they nest, to lower land where food is more plentiful and weather less severe in winter.

Even during the day, **turnstones** feeding on beaches must move with the tides. One of the best times to watch waders is at high tide, when they have been driven off their feeding areas and gather at high tide roosts closer inshore.

The long and short of it

The bills and legs of individual **dunlin** vary in length. The ones with shorter legs and bills are usually those that live furthest north, where it is coldest, because most of their body heat is lost through these unfeathered parts.

CURIOUS CUC

J Robinson (BNHP)

Many people who listen for the well known call of the cuckoo never see one of these slim, long-tailed, grey birds.

Cuckoos spend the winter in Africa and migrate north across the Sahara Desert to Europe, normally arriving in Britain in the middle of April. Because they arrive at the same time as April showers, hearing one is said to be a sign of rain and from this many other superstitions have grown linking cuckoos with good or bad luck.

It is the male bird that makes the familiar 'cuck-oo' call to advertise his territory. Sometimes this changes to 'cuck-cuck-oo' usually during courtship. The call of the female is a less well known, clear bubbling sound, given particularly after egg-laying.

The cuckoo is a brood-parasite, a bird

the species she usually uses. A cuckoo's egg in a robin's nest looks different from one in a pied wagtail's nest. This egg matching helps to ensure that the host does not notice the new egg and either push it out or desert the nest.

For their size cuckoos lay small eggs, but they match fairly closely the size of the eggs they mimic. It is not known whether a cuckoo will pick the same host species as its parent did but, as they tend to return to the same area each year, this seems quite likely.

Cuckoo's eggs take an unusually short time to hatch — only about 11 days — so that the young parasite usually hatches a day or two before the host's own eggs. The blind and naked cuckoo then does an amazing thing. Although a host's egg weighs as much as itself, it nudges each egg to the side of the nest and then uses its legs, back and wings to push it up the side of the nest and over the edge. If any of the eggs have hatched, then the young will also be pushed out.

Cuckoos eat mainly insects, taking a wide variety of larvae as well as centipedes, spiders, ants, worms and slugs which they find on or near the ground. Their favourite food is caterpillars and they will gorge themselves on brightly coloured hairy caterpillars which are avoided by other birds because they are unpleasant to eat.

Their migration south begins in July. The young leave about a month later but often remain here until September. Before migration was properly understood, people believed that cuckoos hibernated in tree-stumps, or even that they turned into hawks in winter. This last idea is not so odd as it seems: cuckoos, with their long tails and barred underparts, look very like sparrowhawks.

So next time you hear a cuckoo calling, try to catch a glimpse of it too. Although several people have made long studies of the cuckoo, scientists are still trying to unravel all its secrets.

that lays its eggs in the nests of 'host' species. The foster parents incubate and bring up the young cuckoo instead of their own brood. The female cuckoo watches carefully to find possible foster parents building a nest. She then flies to the nest, removes an egg, lays one of her own in its place and flies off with the host's egg in her bill and eats it. One female will lay between 10 and 20 eggs in a season.

An individual female will always lay eggs of the same colour to imitate those of

SEPTEMBER

With the onset of autumn, we know that the summer migrants will soon be leaving on their long journey south. In fact, some will have left already. Try keeping a note of every day that you see a swallow or a house or sand martin. Then, one day, your diary will be empty and you will realise that they have gone . . .

Now, instead, there are the winter migrants to look forward to, and all sorts of exciting fungi to liven up a woodland walk!

LOOK AT Lapwings

Key facts

Scientific name: *Vanellus vanellus*.
Key features: from a distance looks black and white, but back is dark green. Slender crest on head. Wings look rounded in flight.
When seen: all year.
Where seen: farmland, shores, estuaries, flood meadows, moorland.
Nests: on flat areas of open ground.
Voice: 'pee-wit' call usually given in flight. Similar but longer call given in spring during display flight.
Food: mainly insects, earthworms and other invertebrates.

E Breeze Jones (Bruce Coleman)

A large flock of lapwings wheeling and twinkling in the evening sunlight over a newly-ploughed field is a common autumn sight. You may have seen smaller flocks as early as June; these were birds that had migrated here from Europe.

Lapwings are our commonest plovers and breed all over the British countryside. In spring it is easy to spot the males in their tumbling display flights. Their large, rounded wings make them look like big, black and white butterflies. When courting a female, the male bows to her, holds his wings high, and then fans his tail.

An inquisitive sheep or cow which wanders too close to a lapwing's nest and eggs is chased off by the bird raising its wings and perhaps making short runs at the intruder. Once the eggs begin to hatch, a parent bird will try to lure away a potential predator by running along, flapping its wings or limping, pretending to be injured.

Later on, when the parents are looking after their chicks, the appearance of a fox or crow will cause the male to fly up and dive-bomb the intruder.

Although they belong to the wader family, lapwings hardly ever wade deeply into water or swim. But they do enjoy bathing and will jump into the air afterwards, flapping their wings quickly to dry themselves.

Many of our breeding lapwings migrate to Ireland or France, where the weather is often milder in winter. Lapwings from Scandinavia, Holland and Germany fly here to escape harsher conditions overseas.

As soon as frosts start in autumn, there is a 'rush migration' of lapwings. Their movements are closely linked with the weather — one day in the severe winter of 1981/82, the warden of the RSPB's Radipole reserve in Dorset counted 13,000 lapwings flying westwards in a desperate bid to avoid a snowstorm.

nature notebook

by Peter Newbery

Swifts and cuckoos left in August — except for a few late stragglers — but all other migrants are now heading south. If you visit the south or east coasts, look among the bushes for redstarts and spotted flycatchers feeding on berries and insects to stock up for the long journey ahead.

Birds that we see all year round such as goldfinches, blue tits and starlings are now gathering into flocks. They are joined by birds of the same species from colder countries who find our winter much milder and food easier to find.

Now birds from the far north start to arrive in Britain for the winter. Redwing and fieldfare flocks arrive by night and the 'tseep' call of redwings can often be heard on stil nights.

Insect food may become short in the winter but berries of wild plants such as lords-and-ladies, hawthorn and holly are important food for birds. Woodpeckers and nuthatches search out hidden insects such as gall wasp larvae.

Female gall wasps lay their eggs in leaves or buds of trees and shrubs. These parts of the plant then develop into many strange shapes. Wild rose buds grow into a red, hairy mass called a robin's pin-cushion. Oak leaves develop blisters on their undersides, called spangles and oak buds change into spongy oak-apples or the common, woody oak-marbles.

If you find an oak-marble on the ground, you will usually find a small hole where the adult wasp has emerged after living its early life as a larva feeding on the woody material of the gall. You may find oak-marbles with no hole still on the tree. Inside is a small grub waiting for the right time to emerge.

Alan Harris

FOCUS on a community

This hedge is teeming with life. All the creatures in it need other living things: to eat, for protection, to help them breed. Together all these living things use each other and so form a community.

Why are these particular species together in this hedge? The sparrowhawk, for example, is here because it can swoop easily from cover onto the chaffinch. The chaffinch, usually a seed eater, is eating large numbers of looper caterpillars. The caterpillars like to feed on hawthorn leaves. The hawthorn was planted here by man.

When you wind up a clockwork toy you give it energy to move. In the same way the community in the hedge would wind down without energy.

These creatures eat each other to get the energy they need to carry on living and breeding. They form a food chain.

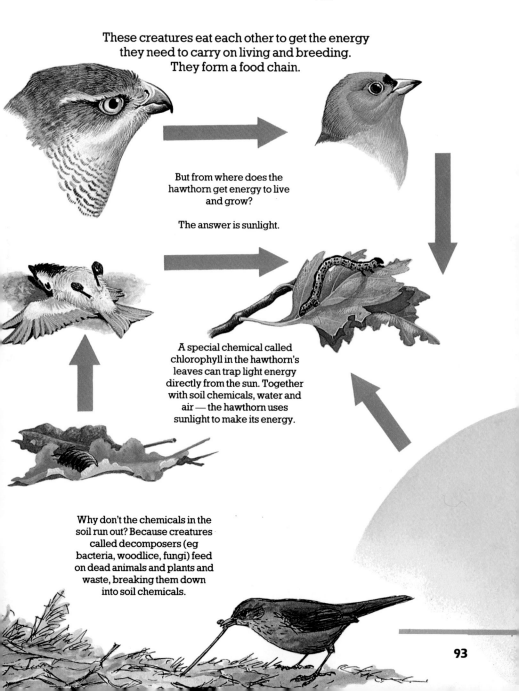

But from where does the hawthorn get energy to live and grow?

The answer is sunlight.

A special chemical called chlorophyll in the hawthorn's leaves can trap light energy directly from the sun. Together with soil chemicals, water and air — the hawthorn uses sunlight to make its energy.

Why don't the chemicals in the soil run out? Because creatures called decomposers (eg bacteria, woodlice, fungi) feed on dead animals and plants and waste, breaking them down into soil chemicals.

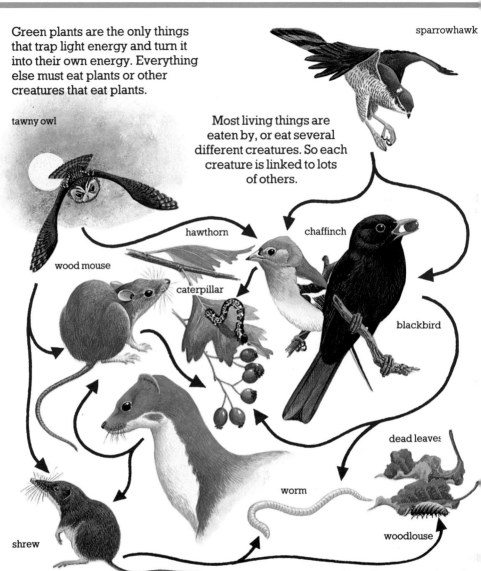

Green plants are the only things that trap light energy and turn it into their own energy. Everything else must eat plants or other creatures that eat plants.

sparrowhawk

tawny owl

Most living things are eaten by, or eat several different creatures. So each creature is linked to lots of others.

hawthorn

chaffinch

wood mouse

caterpillar

blackbird

dead leaves

worm

shrew

woodlouse

These links between living things form a web called a food web. Look back at the hedge and the animals and plants. Pick one and start to draw your own food web.

Imagine removing the hawthorn from this food web. Everything else would disappear. When a hedge is cut down in our countryside the whole community is destroyed.

The living things in the hedge rely on each other for more than just food.

Illustrations by Norman Arlott

Ladybirds use the empty seed pods of red campion as a place to hibernate in winter.

Blackbirds use hawthorn as a place to nest, and feed on the berries in autumn. Hawthorn uses blackbirds to help spread its seeds, scattered in the birds' droppings.

Toads use crevices among the hawthorn's roots to hibernate.

Tufted vetch uses hoverflies to move pollen from flower to flower.

Gall wasps use leaf buds of wild rose to lay their eggs in: the plant reacts by forming prickly 'robin's pin cushion' galls.

Comma butterflies use nettles to lay their eggs on: when they hatch the caterpillars feed on the nettles.

This hedge is a unique community. You can study your own community: in a pond, a tree, a patch of grass — anywhere that a group of animals live. You must first find out what is living there, and then look at how they live together.

You may find that books in the *Spotter's Guide* and *Nature Trail* series (both published by Usborne) will help you identify the living things in your chosen community.

The World of a Hedge by Terry Jennings (Faber) and *The Hedgerow Book* by Ron Wilson (David & Charles) have lots more information about hedge communities.

FUN IN

by Annette Preece

Fungi are fun. They are mysterious, colourful, come in thousands of different shapes and sizes and without them life would soon grind to a halt!

For, together with single-celled creatures called bacteria, fungi recycle all the remains of living things back into chemical in the soil — ready to be used to make the next round of plants and animals.

The colour and shape of the deceiver may vary, hence its name. About 6 cm high, it has a twisted, stringy stem and you can often see white powdery spores on the tawny gills.

King Alfred's cakes are named after the puddings that this king is supposed to have burnt! They are hard and unlike any other fungi. Between 3-6 cm across, they can be seen at any time of year.

What are fungi?

Fungi are rather like plants in the way they are made. But, unlike green plants, they have no chlorophyll and so they cannot make their own food from sunlight and chemicals. Instead, like animals, they feed on dead, or sometimes living animals and plants.

Many fungi, like penicillin and yeast, are tiny and usually go unseen in nature, while others are larger and easy to see, like the mushrooms we buy in the shops. But no matter what they look like, they are all made from a mass of tiny tubes called hyphae (said hi-fee). These tubes form a cobweb mat of strands called a mycelium (my-see-lee-um) — and it is this mat that grows inside the material that the fungus feeds on.

Fungus fruit

The part of a fungus that we usually see is like the flower of a plant, but is better called a fruit body. When two mycelia of the same sort of fungus meet, the hyphae join and grow into a fruit body which produces, not seeds, but microscopic spores.

Circular creepers

The mycelia of many fungi that live in soil grow outwards from their centre in an ever-

FUNGI

increasing circle. Over the years as the edge of the circle grows forwards the middle dies off, making a ring, called a fairy ring. You may have seen those of the fairy ring champignon growing on lawns and pasture. People used to think that they were formed by magic or by lightning, and although we can now explain them scientifically, their sudden appearance still seems to have an air of magic.

Special appearances
The hidden mycelium may not produce fruit bodies every year. Each type of fungus has its own special needs for light, temparature, moisture and food and will only fruit when conditions are just right, so September and October are especially exciting times for the fungus enthusiast!

Fussy fungi
Like anything else, fungi have their favourite foods. Many of them live on dead leaves; some, like sulphur tuft, live on dead wood; while others, such as honey fungus, feed on living trees, eventually killing them.

Spore spreading
Fruit bodies of fungi are a bewildering number of shapes and sizes but they all have one job to do — to spread spores which can grow into a new mycelium. Sometimes the strange appearance of a fruit body is related to how it spreads its spores.

Larger fungi usually have blade-like gills on the underside of their caps where powdery spores are produced and blown away in the wind. The soft, fleshy boletes have tubes instead of gills and so they look like a sponge from below. Puffballs and the rare earthstars produce their spores in their hollow centre and send a puff of spores out through a hole in the top every time a drop of rain hits them.

Velvet shank grows in tufts on dead trees, especially elms, in winter. The stem is yellow near the top, but velvety-brown at its base — giving the fungus its name.

Many-zoned polypore has bands of colour on its velvety upper surface and tiny white pores on its lower surface. It grows on trees and stumps, sometimes in huge clusters.

99

OCTOBER

October can be a glorious month. The trees and hedges have not yet lost their leaves and their rich colours of gold, russet and brown mingle with ripening berries and seeds that are such a valuable source of food for birds. Some fruits such as the vivid red hawthorn berries, rosehips and the waxy red 'cones' of yew are very obvious. Others, such as ash keys and hornbeam seeds are less noticeable, but just as important. Study the different kinds of fruits and berries on your favourite walk this autumn, then as the season progresses you can keep an eye open for the birds that feed on them.

LOOK AT
Goldcrests

Bruce Coleman (Bruce Coleman)

Key facts

Scientific name: *Regulus regulus*
Key features: tiny, compact body; slim, pointed bill. Greenish body with orange-yellow crest, two white wing-bars. Very active.
Where seen: mainly coniferous woods, also large gardens or churchyards with cedar or yew trees.
Nests: under thick cover towards end of branches in conifers; sometimes against tree trunk in ivy.
Voice: high-pitched, thin 'zee'. Song heard from March to early July and mid-August to mid-November.
Food: insects and spiders.

Although goldcrests stay in the British Isles all year, from now until November others from the colder parts of Europe will be arriving on the east coast to winter here.

Weighing only about five grams — half as much as a blue tit — the goldcrest is Britain's smallest bird. In spite of this, birds from northern and eastern Europe manage to migrate across the North Sea in the hope of finding milder weather. The sight of tiny, tired goldcrests arriving on the Suffolk coast each autumn caused local people to name them 'tot o'er seas'.

Goldcrests make this difficult journey because they cannot survive the hard winter weather at home which makes their insect and spider food impossible to find. Even in Britain, more than 50 per cent of goldcrests may die during a hard winter. Fortunately, they can recover from a drop in their numbers quite quickly by raising large numbers of young in the spring. They lay seven to 11 eggs two or three times a year, in a tiny basket of moss hanging by strands of cobweb that hardly look strong enough to support the weight of such a large family!

Because goldcrests prefer conifers, they have been helped by the increase in commercial conifer forests in Britain. They spread to new areas, such as the Shetlands and Scilly Isles, when conifer trees were planted there. In western Britain — especially in Ireland where they are more common — goldcrests may also be found in sessile oak woods.

Agile feeders, goldcrests flit high up in the branches and can hover to catch flying insects, or hang upside down like tits to pick off insects from the underside of leaves. In winter they often move out of conifer woods and feed with tit flocks. Goldcrest song can be hard to hear for older birdwatchers — it is so high-pitched that it is best picked up by young people with perfect hearing!

nature notebook

Autumn is here and in woodlands there is a final flurry of activity as the birds and animals prepare for the cold to come. Leaves will soon be falling and the first frost warns of the coming winter.

the cold, misty mornings. This is the time to listen for the rattling 'chack-chack-chack' of the first fieldfares as they arrive from their northern summer.

The woods are now quiet and the only song to be heard is the robin's, whose sweet autumn notes brighten

Burdock, sorrel, hawthorn and most other plants have finished flowering and now bear a good supply of seeds and berries needed as a source of food for birds, which take advantage of the glut while it lasts.

The ivy, however, is now flowering at its best and is the only source of nectar to be found by late flying insects, which cover its small green flowers. It is particularly attractive to wasps which are very fond of sweet things. They will seek out the ivy blossom when all other supplies are gone.

This is one of the best times of the year to look for fungi, with many different types to be found in the woods. Look out especially for the fly agaric which is perhaps the brightest of all, with its white stem and bright scarlet cap dotted with white scales. Be careful though — this one is poisonous.

Deep in the wood badgers are getting ready for the coming winter when food will be scarce and the nights cold. Extra bedding is collected into bundles and dragged by the badgers, bottom first, into the sett. Feeding now is very important because badgers do not hibernate and there will be days when they cannot find food. So putting on a thick layer of fat now is essential if they are to survive until spring.

Text by R. Petley Jones. Artwork by M. Hodgson.

FOCUS on finches

by Chris Harbard

Eleven species of finch are commonly found in Britain, although the brambling is mainly a winter visitor.
Chaffinch, Linnet, Brambling, Twite, Hawfinch, Redpoll, Greenfinch, Crossbill, Goldfinch, Bullfinch, Siskin.

Finches feed in different ways and have specially shaped bills to suit their food type.

Hawfinch — has a huge, conical bill for cracking hard stones in fruits.

Goldfinch — has a long, narrow bill for extracting small seeds from seed heads.

Bullfinch — has short, rounded bill for picking off buds and breaking ash keys.

Linnet (left) and greenfinch (right) have short, broad bills for picking seeds from the ground.

Illustrations by Rob Hume

Chaffinch — has a large, long bill for eating both seeds and insects.

Redpoll — has short, broad bill for picking small seeds from seed heads.

Crossbill — has a specially designed bill for extracting seeds from cones.

On the wing

Chaffinches, siskins, greenfinches and bramblings from northern Europe migrate to Britain each autumn, joining our resident birds for the winter. Some years, large numbers of **crossbills** fly to Britain for autumn and winter and may even stay to breed. Their specialised feeding habits mean that when their food becomes scarce in the north, large numbers of them have to swarm south in search of a new supply. Such an invasion is called an irruption.

W Lankinen (Bruce Coleman)

Nicknames

Local names for many finches illustrate different aspects of their lives. The goldfinch is called a 'thistle tweaker', the hawfinch a 'cherry finch' and the bullfinch a 'bud picker', each named after the foods they like. The chaffinch is a 'spink' and the redpoll a 'chitty' after their calls; and the **linnet** is a 'gorse bird' and the twite a 'heather lintie' after their favoured habitat.

M C Wilkes (Aquila)

Egg matters

Siskins and **hawfinches** have the shortest incubation period of any British bird, averaging 11-12 days. Predation on eggs and young finches may be high, especially earlier in the season when leaves are not thick enough to cover the nest well. In a study of linnets 68 per cent of nests in bushes were lost to predators in April/May, falling to 46 per cent in July/August.

Slow change

As well as an autumn moult into dull winter plumage, many birds moult again in spring so that they have fresh, bright feathers to attract a mate. Finches, however, moult only once a year in the autumn into dull winter plumage. The bright breeding dress of the males appears by gradual wearing of the dull feather tips to reveal the bright colour below.

Foot facts

Finches vary in the way they use their feet in feeding. Chaffinches and bullfinches never use their feet, while linnets and greenfinches use them to steady food items on the ground. A stage further, siskins, redpolls and **goldfinches** feeding in alder trees will reach to pull in a catkin with their beak, and then anchor it against the branch with their feet while they pick out the seeds.

Not so silent majority

The **chaffinch** is one of the commonest birds in Britain with over seven million pairs estimated in 1976. The songs of individual chaffinches vary slightly, which allows males to recognise each other and females to find their mate. Where birds are separated by a physical barrier such as a mountain, their songs vary even more.

Hence a chaffinch's song from one Scottish glen can be told from that of a bird in a neighbouring glen.

E Duscher (Bruce Coleman)

goldfinch

bullfinch

Look alikes?

Immature goldfinches and bullfinches can be confusing, as they do not have the distinctive head patterns of the adults. The goldfinch lacks the red face, while the bullfinch does not have the smart black cap.

Fruit & Nut Cases

Fruit, nuts and berries are ripening in woods, hedgerows and gardens now — and some birds are making the most of this autumn feast.

K Taylor (Bruce Coleman)

Goldfinches prefer the fruits of plants in the daisy family such as thistle, ragwort and this teasel which provides food in late autumn.

Acorns are a favourite of jays. They often bury them and are said to have a good memory for finding their hidden stores.

R Wilmshurst (Bruce Coleman)

Although woodpigeons feed mainly on our food crops, they may turn to eating acorns, beech nuts and berries in autumn.

Redwings are mainly winter visitors and feed on berries and fallen fruit when they arrive here in October.

NOVEMBER

One of the most exciting sights of a winter's afternoon is watching birds coming into roost. Starlings are well known for gathering in vast numbers and you may have watched them speeding in dark waves over the fields or rooftops to their roosting place, which is often in the middle of a town. But look out for other birds, such as pied wagtails, corn buntings and finches, and don't forget, large roosts attract predators too, perhaps a late-hunting sparrowhawk or an owl!

Roger Wilmshurst (Bruce Coleman Ltd)

Key Facts

Scientific name: *Turdus pilaris*
Key features: size of blackbird; pale grey rump, grey head, black tail, orange chest. White flash under each wing. Loud, rattling calls.
Where seen: mixed farmland with trees and hedges.
When seen: September to April.
Voice: loud, chuckling *'chak-ak-ak'* and lapwing-like *'wee-eep'* in flight.
Food: berries, insects, worms.

Fieldfares arrive from Scandinavia in thousands on the east coast in autumn and quickly spread right across Britain. They flock together to feed on hawthorn berries, rotten apples and other fruits until the trees and hedgerows are bare, when they move into the fields. They keep high in bushes or trees or out on open ground, not skulking about in hedge-bottoms or under bushes like blackbirds. Very often, all the birds in a flock will be facing one way. They like old meadows where they can forage on the grass but also need trees or tall hedges to fly into when disturbed. Then their loud chattering calls attract attention. In mixed thrush flocks moving overhead they can be picked out by their deeper, more nasal flight calls than those of blackbirds or redwings.

Flocks roam from place to place in search of food. Sometimes thousands may be seen passing over to escape frost and snow. They prefer open, soft pastures on which to search for food and hard weather affects them severely.

Fieldfares have gradually spread westwards as breeding birds in Europe and some have nested in Britain since 1967. But they have never become regular breeders and you are unlikely to see a fieldfare in the summer. But they are common and widespread winter visitors and may even come into gardens in bad weather if you put out a few old apples.

nature notebook

by Andrew Simpson

The real start of winter, the hardest time of the year for all our birds and animals, comes in November and December. The short days mean less time to feed and although you may be able to get close to birds, you must be careful not to disturb them. Every second spent feeding is valuable.

The robin has its 'Christmas Card' appearance and looks very plump. Some people think this is because they have been over eating, but they simply fluff out their feathers to give extra protection against the cold winter weather.

Many birds flock together at this time of year. Flocks of finches fly round the countryside searching for food. Look carefully at them. You may be able to spot the orange and white patches of a brambling feeding with chaffinches and greenfinches.

The YOC's own bird, the kestrel, has to work hard to find enough prey to survive. Any mouse or vole which shows itself is in great danger.

In the farmer's fields flocks of plovers can be seen. The lapwing is one of the most spectacular fliers in the bird

world. Its close relative, the golden plover, joins the black-headed gulls, now in their winter plumage, in a constant search for food.

wash up many interesting things on the beach and you may be able to find crabs, starfish and many different kinds of seaweed.

By now you should be feeding the birds near your house. Keep a record of which birds visit your garden. You may be surprised just how many you can see from your windows at home.

Winter is often the best time to explore at the seaside. If you wrap up warmly you can often have the whole beach to yourself. The winter storms

Illustrations by Hilary Burn

FOCUS on owls by Irene Allen

There are about 135 species of owls in the world: from the tiny North American elf owl (13 cm) that breeds in holes drilled in cacti by woodpeckers, to the huge eagle owl (71 cm) that can kill foxes and young deer. Five species regularly breed in Great Britain, while another, the snowy owl, bred in Shetland between 1967 and 1975.

The owl's appealing looks are rather misleading. The very features that attract us make it an efficient hunting and killing machine:

Eyes — large and forward facing to see in poor light and judge distances at night. So big they cannot be moved — instead whole head swivels, sometimes through 270°.

Strong, hooked bill — does not obstruct vision but can tear prey.

Large wings for such a light body help noiseless flight and manoevrability.

Facial disc — saucer-shaped disc of feathers around face that can change shape and may help to funnel sound to the ears which lie behind.

Huge ear openings — pick up very small sounds. Covering flaps change shape to concentrate the owl's hearing in one direction.

Loose, soft plumage — covers quite, a small, light body. Soft, finely fringed feathers deaden the sound of flight.

Feathers on legs — help protect against bites from prey.

Strong legs and toes — with talons for grasping and tearing prey.

Barn owl

John Davies

Bars and stripes

R Siegal (Aquila)

For undisturbed and safe daytime sleep, owls rely on a camouflage of streaked and barred plumage which breaks their outline so they blend in with trunks and branches. Barn owls with their lighter, more noticeable colouring hide away in dark corners and holes.

Long-eared owls blend well with the coniferous trees in which they roost. When alarmed, they stretch upwards and raise their ear tufts so they resemble a broken branch.

A voice in the dark

The sharp 'hee-wick' of the noisy **tawny owl** is just one of its many calls. Night owls are much more vocal than day-flying species, because they rely mainly on sound for communication in the dark. Although so different from the songs of small birds, the mournful 'hooting' of the tawny owl is also used for proclaiming a territory and attracting a mate in the darkness. Barn owls have several calls but do not need a song — their ghostly white shape shows up well at night.

Werner Curth (Ardea)

Pelletable!

It is easy to find out what owls eat because they usually swallow their prey whole. They then get rid of all the inedible parts like fur, bones and feathers, which are passed through the bill as pellets. By examining these you can discover the species of owl which left them and its prey. Research into the prey of the tawny owls in a wood showed 60 per cent of their diet was wood mice and bank voles but they also ate common shrews, young rabbits, moles and beetles. However, their diet varies according to season and area.

Silent hunters

Owls use eyes and ears to find their prey in two main ways. A woodland owl, like the tawny owl waits and watches for rodents or insects from a perch. It hunts in its own familiar territory and tunes its keen sense to detect the smallest sound or movement. Hunting on the wing is the other way of finding food. The **short-eared owl** is a bird of open country, and hunts by flying slowly and pouncing. The barn owl used both these hunting methods, while the little owl often lands on the ground to pursue insect and other prey on foot.

David Hosking

R T Mills (Aquila)

First come, first served

Most owls lay eggs at two-day intervals and start incubating as soon as the first has been laid; so they hatch at different times like these **long-eared owl** chicks. Older chicks are fed first, so if there is not enough food to go round the younger ones die of starvation, leaving more chance of the others surviving.

Friend not foe

The **little owl** is not a native British bird and was introduced into England in the late 1800s. It quickly became unpopular with gamekeepers who blamed it for taking gamebird chicks. An investigation of its pellets by the British Trust for Ornithology, showed its diet to be mainly beetles, earwigs, cockchafers and weevils; not only proving the little owl's innocence but its value to farmers in killing pests.

Flying cats

Barn owls used to be very common and were welcome on most farms where they killed rats and mice which ate the grain. Many old barns had special nestboxes or holes for barn owls. During this century numbers have dropped for several reasons which may include changes in farming, which have reduced rodent numbers and numbers of barns in which they can nest. In some places numbers may have fallen as a result of eating harmful agricultural pesticides in their food. They are now given special proctection under Schedule I of the Protection of Birds Act.

DO NOT DISTURB

Many animals and plants avoid the problems of winter by becoming inactive and hiding until spring. If you discover a sleeping animal, do not disturb it. To wake it up early may cause its death.

1 The slow worm, a legless lizard, hides in holes or under stones.

2 Older frogs prefer to bury themselves in the mud at the bottom of a pond.

3 Many moth pupae rest in the soil until spring when they turn into a winged adult.

4 A hole lined with dead leaves is the hedgehog's winter home.

5 Special winter buds of frogbit rest at the bottom of the pond. In spring they start to grow into new plants and float to the surface.

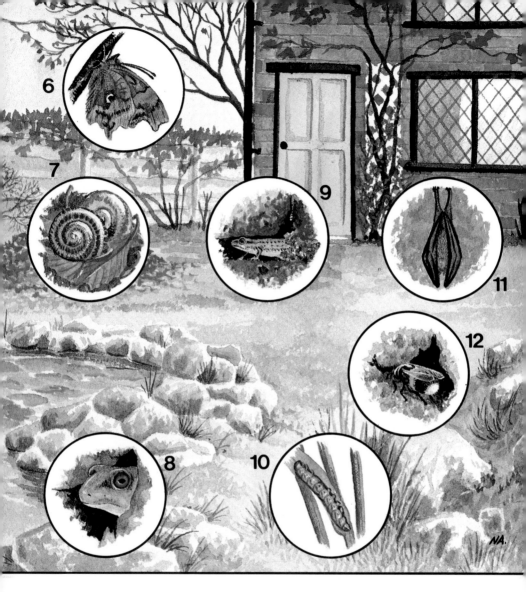

6 Comma butterflies hide on branches where they look like dead leaves.

7 Garden snails contract into their shells and close the opening with several layers of mucus.

8 Toads hide under stones or in old mouse holes.

9 Smooth newts cannot dig holes as their limbs are too weak. They hide in cracks and crevices. Cellars are a favourite place to hibernate.

10 The caterpillar of the angle shades moth rests on a plant stem. In spring it will turn into a pupa, then a flying adult.

11 Tucked away in a corner of roofs or cellars the pipstrelle bat hangs until March.

12 Only the queen bumble bee survives the winter. In spring she will lay her eggs and start a new colony.

DECEMBER

The robin's soft, sweet song can be heard on even the coldest, darkest days of winter. It is a cheering sound and the robin's tame and confiding nature is a great reward for regularly putting out food for birds. Garden birds will come to rely on the food you provide so make sure you top up your bird table every day. The best times to feed the birds are early in the morning and about half an hour before darkness falls. Remember to provide water as well and ensure that during freezing weather it is kept free of ice.

LOOK AT JAYS

Roger Wilmshurst (Bruce Coleman)

This smart jay looks as if he's had his nose in some pastry!

Any kind of fat, meat, cake or nuts might attract a jay to a bird table. Woods are where jays usually live, but they are also in town parks where they can hide away in thick trees. They are bold enough to live near man, but still try to keep out of sight if people are around.

In autumn, jays eat large quantities of acorns, pulling them off the oaks. When they have had their fill, they still take more away and hide them — as many as 2,000 each! During the winter, if food is short, they can find a nice acorn from their autumn store, even if it is covered with snow. Just as important, they pull up seedlings from their planted acorns in the summer, to feed the sprouting (but still whole) acorn to their young.

Except when they are carrying acorns about in the autumn, you might not often see jays, but if you walk through a wood, you will probably hear their loud calls.

Because they need big trees, they are rare in moorland areas, the fens and parts of Scotland and Ireland. They are found all year round in the rest of the British Isles and some more arrive for the winter from the continent.

Key facts
Scientific name: *Garrulus glandarius.*
Key features: Pink; black, blue and white wings, black tail, white rump.
Where seen: Present all year.
Voice: Loud, harsh screech.
Food: Acorns and other fruits, insects, also young birds, eggs, mice.

119

nature notebook

by Peter Bowyer

RSPB education officer at Lochwinnoch in Scotland

The place is a river estuary in early December, near Lochwinnoch Scotland. Flocks of waders wheel round the skies before alighting on the mud to search for food with their probing beaks. Tiny, brown and white ringed plovers scurry along the tideline, mixing with the larger redshanks and godwits, while curlews, with their long, down-curved beaks progress at a more leisurely pace, probing purposefully into the mud for lugworms.

The marshes next to the estuary are good places for wigeon, which graze on the shorter grasses, and often mingle with migrant geese such as whitefronts.

Further inland finches have gathered into flocks to forage on farmland, especially corn stubble, for fallen grain and other seeds. A close look reveals two bramblings, winter migrants from Scandinavia, mixed in with the chaffinches and greenfinches.

easily seen at night, where there are trees. Although its colour blends with its background, I spotted one resting on tree trunks in the day.

A pair of bullfinches are in the hedgerow and chaffinches, greenfinches and a brambling are looking for seeds.

A flash of white in the undergrowth gives away the stoat as it scurries off. Reddish-brown in summer, stoats in northern Britain moult into a white coat for the winter. This acts as better camouflage when snow and ice cover the ground.

In the same hedge, nearby, redwings and fieldfares are eating hawthorn berries.

The winter moth, one of our commonest moths, hatches in October and November and is most

Illustrations by Hilary Burn

121

FOCUS on robins by David Elcome

YOC members' favourite bird, the tame, cheery-looking robin is a tough, aggressive character.

Scientific robin

'Solitary little red bird' is the meaning of the robin's scientific name, *Erithacus rubecula*. Robins are very much lone birds — males and females part as soon as breeding is over to set up territories on their own for autumn and winter.

M Hodgson

War paint

As pretty as it may seem, a robin's red breast is mainly a warning signal. If one robin invades another's territory, the owner puffs out its breast to make the 'red flag' bigger, sways from side to side, flicks its tail and wings and gives a loud burst of song. All this adds up to the message 'Go away or you will be attacked'. This instinct is so strong that robins have been known to attack a red jumper on a washing line and even the red comb on a bantam's head.

M W Richards (RSPB)

Robin sick?

Home sick Britons throughout the world gave the robin's name to other red-breasted birds, like this American robin — which is really more closely related to our blackbird.

Take your partners

Around Christmas time a male robin starts to sing loudly to attract a female. Together they defend a territory, but show little courtship display. In spring, however, the male will courtship feed the female: this probably helps to build up her reserves of body fat ready for the demanding task of producing and incubating eggs.

Birds apart

Originally birds of deciduous woods, robins are now better known in gardens and parks. However, continental robins are still shy birds of thick woodland and look paler than the British and Irish race. Many of them migrate through Britain and a few stay here as winter visitors.

Rob Hume

Christmas robins

Victorian postmen wore red waistcoats and so were nicknamed 'robins'. As the habit of sending Christmas cards grew, the bird soon became popular on the cards delivered by the 'robins'.

Legend says that a robin plucked a thorn from Jesus' crown at the Crucifixion, but in doing so it pierced its own breast. The red stain has remained ever since — a reminder of its kindness.

Roger Wilmshurst

Surprise nests

Old kettles, watering cans, bottles, boots and even a cat skeleton are just some of the places where robins have nested. One pair even built a nest in a bedroom on an unmade bed! Another nested on a horse-drawn wagon which made a return journey of 100 kilometres just after the young had hatched. One parent followed and managed to keep the young fed throughout the journey!

Eric Hosking

M Hodgson

Defenders

A pair of robins defend a territory about the size of a football pitch by song and display. This is probably the largest area they can protect to supply enough food for themselves and their young. In July and August adult robins seem to disappear. In fact they have given up their territories and are quietly moulting. After moult many females will migrate, some as far as Spain. Males and remaining females set up small winter territories.

Roger Tidman

Grow up . . . go away

If young robins had red breasts, they would not only be easy for predators to see, but would probably be attacked by their own parents. The red appears when the young moult in July or August; then they are threatened and chased off by the adults.

Life and death

If all five eggs of both broods of each pair of robins survived we would soon be knee-deep in robins! Instead, many die in their first three months and most live little longer than a year. The oldest known, wild robin was an Irish bird that lived for eleven years. Cats probably kill 40 times more garden robins than do other predators such as owls, kestrels, stoats and rats.

Hans Reinhard (Bruce Coleman)

wrong ways

The birdwatchers in this picture have not seen many birds.
Can you see where they are going wrong? The answers are printed below. Check them for yourself after you have studied the picture.

1. Shouting.
2. Waving hands, binoculars and telescope from inside the hide.
3. Skimming stones on the pond.
4. Taking eggs.
5. Handling young birds.
6. Photographing at the nest.
7. Hide door left open, making occupants visible to the birds on the pond.
8. Dog off lead.
9. Standing on skyline, in front of sun and so scaring off birds.
10. Throwing litter.
11. Going on to private land.
12. Brightly coloured clothes.
13. Binoculars held with strap dangling and not round neck.

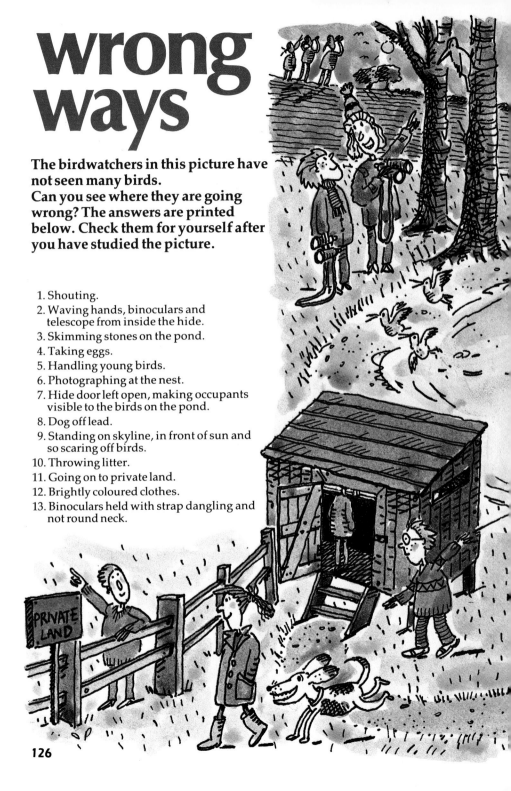

PRIVATE LAND

127

The Young Ornithologists' Club is the junior branch of the Royal Society for the Protection of Birds. With over 85,000 members it is the largest conservation organisation for young people in Europe.

As well as receiving the club's magazine, *Bird Life*, six times a year, members can join in local group meetings and outings, competitions and projects. For a free copy of *Bird Life*, and membership details, please write to the Young Ornithologists' Club (1664), The Lodge, Sandy, Beds, SG19 2DL.

The Royal Society for the Protection of Birds is one of the world's leading conservation organisations. With a fast-growing membership, its aim is to encourage conservation of wild birds by developing public interest in their beauty and place in nature. Its work includes scientific research, enforcement of protection laws, management of over 100 reserves, and education work, including film production and publishing. The Society has a membership of over 390,000. For a free copy of the Society's quarterly magazine, *Birds*, and membership details please write to The Royal Society for the Protection of Birds (1664), The Lodge, Sandy, Beds, SG19 2DL.

Contributors

Geoffrey Abbott	Rob Hume	
Irene Allen	Audrey Lincoln	
John Andrews	Chris Mead	
Peter Bowyer	Peter Newbery	
Tim Cleeves	Robert Petley-Jones	
John Day	Annette Preece	
David Elcome	Steve Rooke	
Nicholas Hammond	Andrew Simpson	
Chris Harbard	Sylvia Sullivan	
Peter Holden		

Artists

Norman Arlott
Hilary Burn
John Davies
Robert Gillmor
Alan Harris
Michael Hodgson
Rob Hume
Mick Loates
John Paige
Chris Shields
Paula Youens